Militarization in the Non-Hispanic Caribbean

WITHDRAWN

Militarization in the Non-Hispanic Caribbean

edited by
Alma H. Young & Dion E. Phillips

Lynne Rienner Publishers, Inc. • Boulder, Colorado

Published in the United States of America in 1986 by
Lynne Rienner Publishers, Inc.
948 North Street, Boulder, Colorado 80302

Library of Congress Cataloging-in-Publication Data

Militarization in the non-Hispanic Caribbean.

Bibliography: p.
Includes index.
1. Caribbean Area—Armed Forces. 2. Arms race—
Caribbean Area—History—20th century. I. Young,
Alma H. II. Phillips, Dion E.
UA609.M55 1986   355'.0330729   86-13019
ISBN 0-931477-78-6

Distributed outside of North and South America and Japan by
Frances Pinter (Publishers) Ltd, 25 Floral Street,
London WC2E 9DS England. UK ISBN 0-86187-656-3

Printed and bound in the United States of America

The paper used in this publication meets the minimum
requirements of the American National Standard for
Permanence of Paper for Printed Library Materials
Z39.48-1984.

Contents

Tables and Figures

Preface

This volume is a first of its kind because it looks specifically at the security issues facing the non-Hispanic Caribbean. We wish to inform a debate that is being waged about the degree of instability in the Caribbean and the role of the United States in helping to fill this perceived political and economic vacuum. The perceived vacuum in the Eastern Caribbean is of special concern to the United States, as recent events in Grenada demonstrate. The emphasis on security issues in the non-Hispanic Caribbean is historic and its impacts can be chilling.

The book is an outgrowth of a panel on "National Security and the Military in the Non-Hispanic Caribbean" presented at the Ninth Annual Meeting of the Caribbean Studies Association in St. Kitts, May 28–31, 1984. All the chapters have been substantially revised and updated, and one chapter was commissioned exclusively for this volume.

The contributors have all done extensive field work in the Caribbean and are aware of the longer and larger historical picture. The perspectives presented here are probing, analytical, and informed by a sense of history. Once again we thank the contributors for their cooperation in meeting the tight deadlines required for a topic of this nature. We appreciate the bibliographic assistance of David Schwam-Baird, and we would like to extend special thanks to Beryl Ochoa, Charles Boyd and Elaine Chapoton who maintained inexplicable good humor despite a trying job of typing and retyping the manuscript.

— The Editors

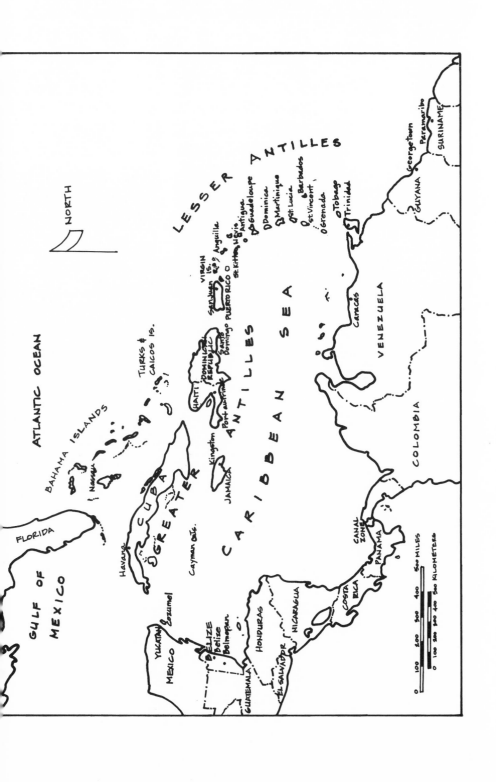

1

Toward an Understanding of Militarization in the Third World and the Caribbean

Dion E. Phillips and Alma H. Young

The year 1979 held much significance for the Caribbean. In March Maurice Bishop and the New Jewel Movement toppled the Gairy government in Grenada. In July the Frente Sandinista de Liberación Nacional (FSLN) defeated the Somoza dictatorship in Nicaragua. Ever since the emergence of these revolutionary regimes, both products of domestic turmoil, and the subsequent cordial political and material relations between these two countries and Cuba, the Caribbean has witnessed a spectacle of frenzied preoccupation with security matters and arms development. The takeoff in the current process of militarization in the Caribbean can be traced back to October 1, 1979 (Taylor 1984:16). Then U.S. president Jimmy Carter, on the pretext that Cuba harbored a "Soviet brigade," set up a new Joint Caribbean Task Force headquartered at Key West, Florida and stepped up electronic surveillance and monitoring of Cuban and Soviet movements.

Since then Washington has treated the Caribbean waters as a U.S. territorial sea and has mounted elaborate shows of sea, air, and land forces to demonstrate the U.S. government means business in the Caribbean. U.S. military assistance to the Caribbean (including the training of security forces) increased sevenfold between 1979 and 1983 (Barry, Wood, and Preusch 1984:196).

In the aftermath a new cold war gripped the Caribbean and with it a new emphasis on militarization. The move to militarize was most dramatic in the non-Hispanic Caribbean where there was little history of the military as a political force. Thus, it was a crucial development when Barbados sent troops to the rescue of the government of St. Vincent on December 16, 1979, following a minor uprising by Rastafarians on Union Island, one of the St. Vincent Grenadines. The late Barbadian prime minister Tom Adams defended the action, warning that developments in the Caribbean dictated that friendly nations help each other. He also argued that military assistance should be regarded as a watershed in the region because for the first time such assistance was sought from within the region rather than from outside (Diederich 1984:11).

The events of 1979 were followed by the military's seizure of power in Suriname in early 1980 and the October 1983 coup in Grenadä, which led to the first U.S. military intervention in an English-speaking island and the first in the region since 1965.[1] Some have argued rather convincingly that the events in Grenada demonstrate that the English-speaking Caribbean, long thought of as the bastion of democracy and civility, is as susceptible to military coups and a militarized society as is Latin America.[2] Governments in the region continue to point to the 1983 coup in Grenada to justify arming and training their respective police forces to protect these same governments from a similar fate. Opposition parties stress that if Bishop had not created an army, he might still be alive. However, the Reagan administration and its conservative allies in the Caribbean have decided that only with armed and well-trained soldiers will these small nations be able to ward off left-wing subversion. Today, as in the past, the boundaries of acceptable sovereign action by Caribbean states have been severely circumscribed by U.S. economic and—whether real or imagined—security interests.

The authors in this volume explore some of the reasons why the non-Hispanic Caribbean states, most of which do not even have regular military units, became militarized almost overnight. The perceived need by the United States for protection of its economic and strategic interests, coupled with the desire by many local governments to quell demands for social change, led to an increasing emphasis on security. The personnel and arms necessary to support the region's security initiatives have escalated in recent years as the United States has poured millions of dollars of military aid into the area. The non-Hispanic Caribbean, once a region characterized by its lack of military institutions, has rapidly become a militarized zone. The implications of this changed status, for individual Caribbean societies and for the region as a whole, are explored in this volume.

The Third World Context: Military Regimes

In the Third World, authoritarian rule has become the norm; governments headed by military men and/or military institutions constitute the most typical variant of this kind of regime. The rise of military regimes has led to a rich literature dealing with the military and its development—for example, the problems of the military in building legitimate authority, the military's capacity to mobilize the citizenry for economic change and to forge grassroots participation, the nature of civil-military relations, and the military's role in creating a country's infrastructure.[3]

In much of this literature the military is viewed as a professional, neutral force whose move into politics is the inevitable outcome of civilian irresponsibility or is a response to a political vacuum created by political and economic instability. The military is also viewed as an important actor in a strategy of orderly development.[4] In reality, the armed forces are powerful political actors with interests and stakes of their own; they operate either individually or in concert with other actors in society. The military is one of many actors within the political system, not a neutral force outside the system's boundaries. When the military enters the political arena, not only are the rules of the game changed by its presence, but the military institution itself is transformed into a highly political institution (Valenzuela 1985:140).

Much of the literature also mistakenly downplays the political impact of foreign influences on the military institutions in terms of training, material support, and the development of strategies that define political action (Valenzuela 1985:141). Yet much of the political role of the military in Central America, for example, grows from the ties between local officers and their U.S. counterparts. Often, rather than being an agent for change, the military sees its role as preserving the status quo. As the military comes to play a more central role in political life, its participation precludes the development of institutions based on accommodation and compromise. Thus change becomes even more difficult to introduce.

Forces That Promote Militarization in the Third World

Militarization, whether in the Caribbean or in other parts of the Third World, refers to the tendency of a national military apparatus (armed forces, paramilitary organizations, intelligence and bureaucratic agencies) to assume increasing visibility, involvement, and control over the social lives and behavior of the citizenry. The process of militarization also encompasses military domination of national priorities and objectives at the expense of civilian institutions. This definition of militarization is consistent with reality in the Caribbean and in other Third World countries where the role of military and paramilitary establishments in national and international affairs is growing, the use of force as an instrument of dominance and political power is increasing, and the influence of the military in civilian affairs is escalating. Hence, the process of militarization is not a static but a dynamic condition involving the progressive expansion of the military sphere over the civilian sphere of the neocolonial state.

To comprehend militarization in the Third World generally requires a conceptual framework that identifies the combination of internal and external conditions that generates and promotes the phenomenon. It is useful to commence this analysis by dichotomizing these general forces into internal factors (those indigenous to a given country) and external factors (those that promote and propel militarization across international boundaries).[5]

Internal Factors

Among the assortment of internal factors that generate and foster militarization are the following:

Maldistribution of wealth. In a given society where a small segment of the population owns a disproportionate share of the nation's wealth, that privileged minority is likely to depend on the use of military force to deter or quell any threats to the status quo. The deposed dictatorship of Jean-Claude Duvalier in Haiti was a classic example of this.

Racial oppression. Similarly, in any society where the people of one race are politically and/or economically subordinated by the people of another race, the dominant racial grouping tends to rely on the use of military force to deter and crush rebellion on the part of the oppressed. Sometimes the entire state apparatus, including the military, is virtually the private property of a very small group. Guyana under the People's National Congress appears to be moving in this direction.

The "national security" obsession. The "national security" obsession is the tendency to expand the concept of national security to include internal security. A large portion of the impetus behind this change in Third World countries often is provided by U.S. military training programs. These programs promote the professionalization of Third World officer corps as well as concentrate on counterinsurgency and civic action. The national security obsession is also often expressed in development terms whereby the military argues that it is the only institution capable of managing rapid economic growth.

Perceived insecurity in the face of external threats. Countries surrounded by hostile neighbors, whether real or imagined, tend to develop a seige mentality that views any unusual external move (military exercises, troop movements, arms acquisition) as an indication of impending hostilities for which appropriate countermeasures must be sought. In many instances, this mentality persists long after the initial threat has dissipated and becomes part of the social fabric.

Maintenance of or increase in the military's share of national resources. Once a society has created a military apparatus in response to some real or imagined threat, this institution will often seek to maintain and even increase its share of national resources. Often, this drive is produced by the desire of the officer class to enhance its status vis-a-vis the traditional ruling class. The armed forces are particularly well placed to press their demands because they have a monopoly on the means of violence. However, security systems do not always have to resort to intervention (for example, coups d'état) to increase their share of national resources. Often, civilian-dominated governments that are dependent on military support or that are faced with opposition from their own military find it prudent to supply the armed forces with the requested resources.

External Factors

Among the range of external factors that promote and sustain militarization in Third World countries are:

Major-power intervention. History is replete with examples of major powers that have sought to protect or expand their empires by dislodging leaders and replacing them with local figures (warlords) who agree to or can be constrained to serve the imperial cause. Although most formal arrangements of this kind are no longer in vogue, in actuality, the practice still obtains in the efforts of the major powers to promote the creation of friendly military elites in the client states of the Third World. Such efforts have long conditioned U.S. policy in the countries of the Third World and constitute the core of Ronald Reagan's new military policy in the English-speaking Caribbean. U.S. support for friendly governments includes arms deliveries, military training, and technical assistance. In some instances (Iran, 1953; Guatemala, 1954; Brazil and the Dominican Republic, 1965; Chile, 1973; Grenada, 1983), U.S. aid and troops have been used to help engineer the collapse of governments and their replacement by pro-U.S. governments.

Major-power entanglement in indigenous conflicts. The major powers usually view conflict in the Third World, regardless of a conflict's source, as having an impact on their global strategic interests. Consequently, the major powers often attempt to influence the outcome of such conflict by providing their respective clients with arms, training, and advice. However, when such support is provided, other parties to the dispute will invariably seek assistance from a competing great power. Moreover, because the major powers tend to measure the status of their security by the fortunes of their clients, they are often disposed to match or even outstrip any arms deliveries made by another great power to their clients' rivals. Predictably, this situation tends to intensify the local arms race and increase the risk of great power entanglement in local disputes.

Cross-national ideological conflict. As history demonstrates, national leaders often feel constrained by ideological ties to provide military assistance to like-minded governments faced with aggression. The polarization of the globe into pro- and anticommunist alliance systems is the hallmark of this phenomenon, although, of course, the socialist world itself is torn by the ideological conflict between the Soviet Union and China. Such ideological affinities ensure that Third World countries often have ready access to modern military equipment and, as a consequence, the task of negotiating a peaceful settlement to local conflict is further complicated.

International marketing of arms. Many developed countries export arms to Third World countries to sustain their own domestic munitions industries. However, an increasing number of nations possess the capacity to produce weapons, and this has resulted in intense competition between the exporters of arms. Such keen competition has led to the adoption of sophisticated sales tactics by arms exporters to induce arms-importing countries to augment military spending. This competition has therefore given rise to an increase in the warmaking capabilities of Third World countries.

Collective security alliances. Collective security alliances in Third World countries are often created in response to real or perceived dangers, but these pacts tend to evolve a life of their own after the original danger has passed. Various governments and/or interest groups often have a vested interest in the maintenance and survival of such collective security arrangements and thus will, if necessary, intervene in the political process of member states to assure the continued commitment and adherence of member states to these alliances.

Convergence of Military Interests

Although it is useful to divide internal and external factors for purposes of description, these factors typically work in concert and reinforce one another. Hence, a comprehensive analysis of the militarization process comprises all these factors, each of which tends to nurture and support the others. Hence, on the one hand, the geopolitical and economic interests of the major powers, as denoted by arms sales to clients, often promote the rise of military institutions within Third World countries; on the other hand, the inclination of Third World military elites to strengthen their position relative to civilian elites often leads the former to forge alliances with the military of the major powers in order to obtain the arms, training, and equipment to carry out their political designs. This coincidence of interests suggests that there is an interdependence of militarism between the major powers (and, in some instances, the "middle powers") and the Third World countries. This interdependence is characterized by some analysts as a world military order in which military developments in any given country or any bloc of countries tend to be related to developments in other countries.

The conjunction of all of the above-mentioned factors enhances the power of the state in Third World countries, particularly its military sector relative to other sectors and the general population. As a consequence of this pattern these factors obviously create, promote, and foster militarization in the countries of the Third World, of which the Caribbean is an integral part.

Forces That Generate Caribbean Militarization

To understand the tendency toward reshaping the role of the military in the Caribbean in the postindependence period requires an identification of those forces, both external and internal, that generate and promote the need for an increased emphasis and dependence on security in the region. At the end of World War II the United States emerged as unquestionably the strongest power in the world. However, by the end of the late 1960s/early 1970s there was a marked decline in U.S. economic, military, and political power. The objective weakening of U.S. economic strength had its impact on the Caribbean.

Because economic development in the eyes of the Caribbean ruling classes means capitalist development based on the ascendance of capital led by U.S. multinational corporations, when these corporations experienced dislocation in the late 1960s and early 1970s, social and economic problems became rife in the Caribbean. Such problems were evidenced by widespread income inequality in Jamaica, Trinidad/Tobago, Barbados, and Guyana. Unemployment and underemployment levels in these countries ranged from 25 to 50 percent, inflation ranged between 10 and 32 percent, and foreign exchange problems were prevalent. In the ministates of the Eastern Caribbean, where the level of industrialization and productivity is even lower, the social and political reality was even grimmer (Inter-American Development Bank 1980:85).

Consequently, the deep-seated economic and social crisis in the Caribbean, which occurred at a time when the U.S. international position had weakened and the Puerto Rican model of industrialization by invitation was being questioned as a viable strategy for development, made it impossible for local political directorates to conduct business as usual. This crisis was instrumental in triggering a number of economic, social, and political developments in the postindependence period that worried local elites as well as the United States.

The stability that allegedly characterizes the Westminster-type democracies of the Commonwealth Caribbean began to dissolve in the face of social disorder in Trinidad in the late 1960s and in Jamaica in the early 1970s (Gonsalves 1979; and Shak 1971).[6] These political developments sent shock waves throughout the region (especially in countries where the transition to independent sovereign status was uneventful) and played havoc with the legitimacy and self-confidence of regional governments.

Although the governments of these two leading Commonwealth Caribbean countries were able to subdue the uprisings, the events led to two far-reaching outcomes. First, in the aftermath of this unprecedented unrest there emerged the tendency on the part of local governments to increase their emphasis and dependence on instruments of security. Second, these uprisings encouraged Caribbean governments, particularly Trinidad, Guyana, and Jamaica, to broaden state participation in the economy as a way of addressing the root cause of political instability and coopting future unrest. The immediate effect of state intervention was a tendency to reduce the scope of direct foreign investment and the direct outflow of surplus. Predictably, however, capital responded by limiting its activities in these countries, thus aggravating production (Watson 1982b; Jones 1981). Such actions had a ripple and compounding effect on political instability in the region.

In the late 1970s the Caribbean masses became increasingly politicized, although this was not accompanied by a high level of political mobilization, except in Grenada. In Grenada the openly repressive practices of the Gairy regime, together with that government's inept domestic economic policies, resulted not only in the inevitable alienation of large segments of the population but served to radicalize and galvanize sections of the intelligentsia (through the New Jewel Movement) who denounced Eric Gairy's leadership. These circumstances ostensibly laid the foundation for the March 13, 1979, revolution, which not only dramatically changed the geopolitical climate of the Eastern Caribbean and altered the terms of U.S. cold war politics in the region, but debunked the thesis that Caribbean governments have "control" of the political process.

The other ministates of the Eastern Caribbean began to respond to a state of political ferment rooted in the social and economic ills of the area by empowering progressive and/or radical regimes, as in St. Lucia, St. Vincent, and Dominica. Such regimes emerged at a time when Cuba's popularity was high and collectively the region was becoming curious and increasingly tolerant of its Cuban neighbor to the north. Hence, a select number of the new nation-states of the Caribbean began to form links with the Cuban Communist party and the Cuban state as well as with socialist bloc countries. Even the centrist government of Barbados under Errol Barrow gave tacit approval, in the name of support for African liberation struggles, by allowing Cuban aircraft transporting troops to Angola to refuel in Barbados. Moreover, for the first time in the history of postindependence Commonwealth Caribbean politics, a discussion of socialism appeared on the agenda of Caribbean affairs.

The relative politicization and radicalization of the Caribbean population between 1972 and 1980 were influenced not only by the domestic crisis in each country but by the decline of U.S. hegemony in the world at large and in the Caribbean in particular. During this hiatus, the United States by dint of circumstance was forced to make certain ephemeral and tactical adjustments in its foreign policy. This adjustment was reflected in the Carter administration's tentative embrace of "principles of ideological pluralism" and a "human rights" policy in Latin America and the Caribbean. This opening in the international situation made it possible for Caribbean states to experience "certain degrees of freedom" as exemplified by their greater involvement in Third

World affairs as well as by political developments in Guyana, Jamaica, Nicaragua, and Grenada.

But the 1980s brought a conservative change in the politics of the region with Edward Seaga in Jamaica, Tom Adams in Barbados, George Chambers in Trinidad/Tobago, Eugenia Charles in Dominica, and John Compton in St. Lucia. This full complement of conservative Caribbean leaders would prove to make good political bedfellows for the man in the White House, Ronald Reagan, and his policies, particularly the new interventionist policy with its militaristic thrust (see Dixon 1985).

Response to the Crisis

The decision by state systems in the Caribbean to increase their emphasis and dependence on security, inclusive of which is the reshaping of the role of the indigenous military (defense forces), is largely a response by U.S. policymakers and local elites to what is perceived as a crisis of regional security—that is, the spread of Cuban communist "expansionism" into a weak area as well as the slowly developing crisis implicit in the failure of the economic and social development strategies of the 1960s.

This policy of increased security is based on the assumption that countries of the Third World, including the Caribbean, are largely incapable of immediate and substantive economic transformation and stability. Hence, it becomes necessary to reinforce the security systems of these countries as a prerequisite to their eventual economic development. Put simply, the military is embued with the virtue of being the savior of the system and the agent of crisis management, if need be.

This new role for the military in the Caribbean, a role informed by the current U.S. interventionist foreign policy whose latest expression is embodied in the Caribbean Basin Initiative, constitutes a coincidence of interest between local ruling elites and the Reagan administration in the latter's attempt to reassert U.S. hegemony in the region.[7] It therefore stands to reason that because the U.S. state and private sectors have much at stake in the region, the U.S. government's current preoccupation is with the protection and expansion of those sectors interested in this period of reassertion. Hence, in this schema the military can be used as a countervailing force to deter radical forces from gaining or consolidating power.

Given the geopolitical and economic importance of the Caribbean to the U.S., "instability" in this area is construed by the

United States as threatening to its own security, especially where such instability is likely to serve as a magnet for nonhemispheric intervention or interference. Consequently, when progressive forces and the political left in the Caribbean demanded that the political economies of the region be democratized and that foreign influence in the economic, political, social, and cultural life of these countries be reduced, Washington chose to interpret these trends as part of Cuban- and Soviet-sponsored subversion in the region (especially in light of the revolutions in Nicaragua and Grenada). These trends were not viewed in Washington as products of the inequitable distribution of income and wealth long characteristic of the region and the inability or unwillingness of respective governments to redress these inequities. Hence, the increasing emphasis and dependence on security, part and parcel of which is the rise and expanded role of Caribbean "client armies," are directed at combating this alleged subversion.

Implications Of Caribbean Militarization

The tendency toward militarization in the Caribbean in the postindependence period is corroborated by the inclination of the military to increase its share of national resources (emanating from its role as arbiter) and to absorb excess labor. In so doing the military aids in the maintenance of the status quo and serves as an agent of the restoration of U.S. hegemony.

Increase in State Expenditure for Military Institutions

The creation and permanence of military institutions in the neocolonial Commonwealth Caribbean have had a profound impact on the strategy for economic transformation in these new nation-states. The military, in its support of the state and in its policies, must too be supported. Consequently, there is a tendency on the part of these military organizations to command an increasingly significant share of state (budgetary) expenditure.

The expenditure on military institutions in the Caribbean has been on the increase. For example, between 1972 and 1979 the proportion of expenditure on the military in Trinidad/Tobago, Jamaica, and Guyana not only steadily increased but more than doubled. In the case of Guyana, in particular, such an increase accounted in 1979 for as much as 3.3 percent of the total state expenditure. By 1983 Guyana's expenditure on the military was estimated at 10 percent of the total national budget.

One of the reasons for the rise in public expenditure to the military is the relative "weakness" of regional political parties in mediating domestic conflict, which inevitably springs from domestic crisis. This increasing delegitimization of the respective Caribbean directorates (more in countries such as Guyana) creates a political vacuum for the military sector and sets the stage for the coup and countercoup syndrome, thus ushering in the Central Americanization of the new nation-states of the Caribbean (Erisman 1983).

The Central Americanization of the Caribbean is not unthinkable because military intervention is considered easier to effect in the presence of weak, civilian-dominated governments. Military officers contend that they are constrained and morally required to intervene in politics (take over the government) when civilian governments have proven to be incapable of governing and are unresponsive to the needs of their population—all predictable symptoms of the global economic crisis.

Absorption of Excess Labor

It historically has been the case in Caribbean countries, where unemployment and underemployment are major problems and a clear reflection of the global economic crisis, that the government systematically encouraged and endorsed the emigration of labor to the metropoles of Britain, Canada and the United States. However, such a policy of state-sponsored emigration, a most persistent and superficial way of addressing the crisis, has in recent years come up against the increasing tendency of Britain, Canada, and the United States (the traditional recipients of Caribbean migration) to introduce more stringent requirements for entry (see Marshall 1985; Bray 1985). Moreover, emigration has, in large measure, involved "professional, technical and kindred workers" and therefore excludes a sizable number of school dropouts (youth) who every year join the ranks of the unemployed; these dropouts then become part of the so-called crisis strata and socially explosive elements of these societies. Hence, Caribbean militarization has the latent function of absorbing and disguising a limited supply of jobs and in so doing forestalling the likelihood of progressive elements mobilizing the youth and the unemployed, who have long been known as fertile soil for social unrest.

This limited absorption of the unemployed by Caribbean military institutions is reflected in the growth in the size of the military itself. Between 1978 and 1980 the percentage of the adult population in the armed forces of Jamaica doubled (Sivard 1983). In the case of "socialist" Guyana, the most militaristic of the Commonwealth Caribbean countries, there was a meteoric rise from 2 military personnel for every 1,000 citizens in 1972 to 5 military personnel for every 1,000 citizens in 1979. By 1983 the ratio of military personnel to civilians stood at 1 to 45.

In This Book

Watson (Chapter 2) argues that the myth that the British bequeathed enduring democratic traditions and institutions to their former Caribbean colonies is being shattered as the authoritarian state becomes more commonplace in the Commonwealth Caribbean. The authoritarian state, as reflected in the development of military and security instruments of state power, is a function of the deepening economic and political crises in the area, in which the interests of the ruling classes and of imperialism have come increasingly under attack and the traditional populist strategies have proven inadequate to shore up support for these regimes. The implosion of the Grenada Revolution provides a justification for increasing and strengthening the role of the military and the police in the national life of these societies, and gives U.S. imperialism a golden opportunity to facilitate this process while simultaneously integrating the security instruments into the U.S. system. The real reason for the creation of the security force, Watson suggests, is to dissuade the masses from any political and social action that may be useful in their struggle against exploitation and repression.

The failure of the economic and social development strategies of the 1960s has resulted in the slowly developing crisis of economic and social disorganization now widespread in the Eastern Caribbean. This disorganization breeds resistance movements as domestic groups seek alternative ways of addressing the structural problems confronting their societies. However, indigenous political developments are perceived by U.S. policymakers and local elites as assaults on the status quo and as examples of the spread of Soviet/Cuban ideology. As a consequence of this cold war view of the world, U.S. policymakers in concert with many Eastern Caribbean leaders have decided to increase their emphasis on security and defense matters. Phillips (Chapter 3) argues that rather than providing the conditions for progress and development, the increasing emphasis on security and defense now being seen in the Eastern Caribbean has the effect of serving as a prophylactic against social change; increasing security now is considered the agent of crisis management.

The revolutionary experiment in Grenada had a major impact on the Caribbean. This experiment represented the first coup in the English-speaking Caribbean, thus demonstrating the frailty of the Westminister model in the region. The death of the revolution also demonstrated how violence begets violence, both internally and internationally. Boodhoo argues in Chapter 4 that the assassination of Prime Minister Maurice Bishop and three of his cabinet ministers on October 19, 1983, was the culmination of thirty-five years of steadily increasing levels of violence within Grenada. The violence and the militarization of the society practiced by Eric Gairy led to his downfall at the hands of the New Jewel Movement. Although the Bishop government was relatively successful in meeting many of the basic needs of the population, the use of coercion as a method of control continued. The international determinants of the increased militarization of Grenada, especially the roles played by Cuba, the USSR, and the United States, are highlighted and demonstrate the limited options available to Caribbean regimes interested in creating new political models.

In February 1980 a group of noncommissioned officers, angry that they were not allowed to unionize, overthrew the civilian government of Suriname in a relatively bloodless coup. Almost three years later in December 1982 the military defended the government against an alleged coup attempt by executing fifteen Surinamese opposition leaders. Sedoc-Dahlberg contends in Chapter 5 that the increasing grip by the military on Surinamese society parallels the government's loss of support from major interest groups, especially labor federations and religious organizations. The 1982 executions came as major groups were demanding a return to democracy. The author also documents the increasing degree of military involvement in government decisionmaking, such that by 1984 the cabinet was dominated by representatives of the military. The inability of the government to create new political organizations to replace the ones banned by the regime provided the opportunity for the military to assume a greater role in the society.

Danns (Chapter 6) maintains that in Guyana the regime has relied for years on a broad-based military apparatus to sustain regime rule and to enforce the regime's unpopular measures. Thus, Guyana has emerged as probably the most militarized of

Commonwealth Caribbean countries in terms of the ratio of military personnel to citizens, the proportion of national resources expended on the military, and the number and variety of military institutions. Serious crises of legitimacy, credibility, and accountability confront the state. The military is relied upon to preserve the status quo and impede any democratic succession to the regime. As in Guyana, more governments in the region are acting with armed arrogance and displaying increasing irritation and intolerance with any form of opposition. Although governments are relying increasingly on the military, they are also fearful of possible coups and therefore, as in Guyana, elaborate procedures of divide and rule are instituted to keep the military off guard.

Belize has not been drawn overtly into the violence that is raging throughout Central America, but the escalating crisis in the area reminds Belize that it cannot escape its geographical boundaries. Young argues in Chapter 7 that the Central American crisis is impacting Belize in a number of ways. Thousands of refugees now pour across the Belizean borders. Millions of dollars in U.S. economic and military aid have become available to help stabilize the country. There has also been an increase in the presence of the military; British soldiers serve as a defense against a possible invasion from Guatemala (which claims Belize), and local forces are being used increasingly for national security. The clearest signal that the crisis is impacting Belize is that the country is being drawn more firmly within the U.S. orbit, a circumstance that could lead to a greater Central Americanization of the country.

Whether in Belize, Grenada, or Barbados, the increasing emphasis on militarization has profound implications. It suggests that local military institutions will serve in the 1980s as bulwarks of the status quo and as protectors of U.S. geopolitical and economic interests in the region. Democratization will be stifled as the military comes to see itself as the ultimate mediator of the local political system, and true nationalism will be discouraged as the countries are drawn tighter into the U.S. sphere of influence. As Vaughan Lewis has written, "The emphasis on security is ultimately destructive of the society" (1982:11).

Notes

1. If one considers direct military intervention alone, the Caribbean and Central America have suffered the presence of U.S. troops on their shores and soil more than any other region. The better-known and longer military occupations of this century include: Panama, 1903–1914; the Dominican Republic, 1903, 1905, 1916–1924, 1965–1967; Cuba, 1906–1909, 1912; Honduras, 1907; Nicaragua, 1909, 1912–1925, 1926–1933; Haiti, 1915–1934; and Grenada, 1983.

2. See Gordon Lewis' comments in Diederich (1984); also see Phillips (1985).

3. Among the many articles on these problems, see, especially, Feit (1973); McKinley and Cohan (1973); and Jackman (1976).

For Latin American problems specifically, see Lowenthal (1976); and Solaun and Quinn (1973).

4. See, for example, Finer (1976); Huntington (1968); Perlmutter (1977); Johnson (1962: especially chapters by Pye, Shils, and Halpern); Stephan (1971); Fitch (1977); and Decalo (1976).

5. The following were especially helpful in developing the framework under discussion here: Thee (1977); and Simmons (1985).

6. Westminster-type democracies are those systems of constitutional and political governance bequeathed by Britain to its former colonies and characterized by regular elections, political parties in opposition, separation of legislative and executive branches, and the rule of law.

7. See Watson (1982b). For a discussion of the accumulation needs and requirements of world capitalism, see Watson (1985).

2
Imperalism, National Security, and State Power in the Commonwealth Caribbean: Issues in the Development of the Authoritarian State

Hilbourne A. Watson

This chapter deals with problems related to the development of the postcolonial state in the Commonwealth Caribbean. Indeed, there already is a considerable body of literature on the development and underdevelopment of the state in postcolonial societies,[1] but a study of state development in the Commonwealth Caribbean must address (if it is to be complete) the problem of economic crisis[2] and the phenomenon of imperialism both as a modern form of empire and a stage in the development of capitalism. Thomas (1984) has argued that we are now witnessing the crystallization of an "authoritarian" form of state in the "periphery," and in my judgment this characterization of the state is basically applicable to the Commonwealth Caribbean, with certain modifications.[3]

Although it may surprise the ruling classes in the Commonwealth Caribbean to find its state classified as authoritarian and although U.S. imperialism will certainly object to the classification, this particular state form has been rapidly developing before our very eyes. Most of us have not seen it because our perceptions are shaped by the ideology of the "democratic" state and by the myth that Britain bequeathed enduring democratic traditions and institutions to its former Caribbean colonies. For the most part social science scholarship in the region has had a remarkable tendency to confuse the institution of government with the state. Government is a necessary part of the state and consists of the regime that exercises state power. The state is not reducible to the institution of government, which may change from one election period to another or from one coup d'état to another. The government of Barbados is currently under the control of the Democratic Labour Party, which is headed by Errol Barrow, but the Barbadian state is more than the Democratic Labour Party. Nor is the state reducible to a mere passive instrument of the ruling class. If this were the case, class struggles and revolutions would have no meaningful historical role or function.

17

In this chapter I pay particular attention to the expansion and development of the coercive instruments of state power with special emphasis upon the military and police instruments. My objective is limited: I address what Phillips (1983b) has called the "military and security" arms of the state. This theme has received some attention from Danns (1978, 1982, 1984), Lewis (1982), and Watson (1982a, 1984c). Other observers including Diederich (1984) have drawn attention to this phenomenon, especially after the implosion of the Grenada Revolution and the invasion and occupation of that country by the United States. Although Thomas (1984) does not study the Commonwealth Caribbean in particular, it is clear that many of his empirical referents are drawn from the experience of Guyana.

I argue that the development of the authoritarian state in the Commonwealth Caribbean as reflected in the broadening of the scope of the military and security instruments of state power is a function of the crisis generated by the traditional exclusion of the popular masses from access to and control over the state and related structures. I also argue that the structural crisis of the neocolonial model of capital accumulation, which continues to reproduce weak and precarious economic and political institutions, in the Commonwealth Caribbean is at the hub of the "rise" of this authoritarian state. In this same context, I show that the political ruling class in the Commonwealth Caribbean is led by a petite bourgeoisie that has been unable to reproduce itself outside of the state and that must simultaneously reproduce its control over the state in alliance with local capital, sections of the productive classes, and imperialism.

The model of capital accumulation of which I speak has been based historically upon the ascendance and consolidation of merchant capital, agrocommercial capital, foreign investment in light industry, primary export specialization, and acceptance of, and willing participation in, the imperialist division of labor. As I have indicated elsewhere (Watson 1984a, 1984b, 1984c), agrocommercial capital, which has its roots in merchant capital and plantation agriculture, reinforces and reproduces a structural production bias that undermines the production and augmentation of exchange value and elevates the production and circulation of use values. It also blocks the development of wage labor-capital relation by retarding the development of the productive forces and by maintaining a high import content in local production (which weakens the role of both capital and labor) and, in conjunction with imperialism, creates a situation in which the symptoms of underdevelopment masquerade as its causes (Watson 1984c).

The reproduction of labor power and value becomes the fundamental problem confronting and undermining capital accumulation and capitalist expansion in these societies. Exploitation of labor power is maintained by capital and by the state through repressive policies and practices and juridical norms that legalize and reproduce the uneasy coexistence of backward capital and modern capital: that is, combinations of techniques of absolute and relative surplus value. In order to maintain the social order rooted in these practices, the popular masses, including workers and small farmers (peasants), have had to be held at bay and away from access to state power.

The petite bourgeoisie that currently controls the state as a part of the ruling class has its social class origins mainly outside of capital: in the professions, the bureaucracy, and the trade union movement. This new type of ruling class, which can also be found in other neocolonies, achieved this position with the support, and largely at the expense, of the popular masses. This class must continue to exclude the popular masses from state power in order to reproduce itself and the class alliances and coalitions necessary for the perpetuation of class power and rule. Thus, the natural allies of this class are the traditional agrocommercial capitalists, the coterie of military, bureaucratic, and professional "elites," foreign capital, the major international and regional institutions such as the World Bank Group, Organization of American States, and the Inter-American Development Bank, and imperialism, under the leadership of the U.S. state.

The exploited classes in the Commonwealth Caribbean have not willingly or freely accepted their exploitation and deprivation. The petite bourgeoisie has skillfully used its advantageous position to manipulate, politicize, mobilize, and demobilize the masses; it has been relatively successful in mythmaking, in ideological control, and in the utilization of other techniques necessary for class rule. Central to this process of manipulation, control, and legitimation is the propagation of the myth that these societies are the epitome of Westminster-type democratic systems. In this regard the Commonwealth Caribbean state and its ideologues have equated the form of democracy (the two-party system, regular elections, and a unitary government) with the social and political content of democracy, and there is a cacophony of voices raised to support this myth that is led by U.S. imperialism, which is doing whatever it can to undergird these regimes in this period of crisis.

For example, the United States has devised and implemented, in the form of the Caribbean Basin Initiative (CBI), a restructuring mechanism for responding to the capitalist world economic and political crisis as it affects U.S. interests in the entire Caribbean Basin area.

The CBI is neither a military-strategic program nor simply an economic recovery program. The Initiative incorporates elements of both programs, but it is not reducible to a combination of their components. In order to properly understand what the CBI represents in terms of U.S. national interests it is necessary to situate the CBI in the context of the present global situation and position of the United States. As a restructuring mechanism the CBI is designed to reorganize the U.S. position in the Caribbean Basin. To this end the United States is bent on completing the integration of the region into its domain, and this integration involves economic, geopolitical, and strategic-military processes.

In terms of economics, CBI trade, investment, and aid are intended to provide infrastructure, reduce production costs, discipline Caribbean labor, improve the competitive edge of U.S. capital, and reduce the role of foreign competitors in the region. With respect to geopolitical issues, the CBI is designed to overcome the challenges that regional political instability represent for the United States. The Grenada Revolution (1979-1983), Jamaica's adoption of "democratic socialism" (1972-1980), and the Sandinista Revolution in Nicaragua represent(ed) and open(ed) up possibilities for diversifying the political economy and foreign policy options available to the region. Cuba has been viewed as a major source of support for these options and possibilities.

The electoral defeat of Michael Manley in Jamaica (1980), the overthrow of the Grenada Revolution (1983), the launching of a U.S.-financed and -supported counterrevolution against the Sandinistas in Nicaragua, and the arming and training of security forces throughout the Commonwealth Caribbean (and the entire region) have all contributed to expansion of U.S. political influence and military power in the area. The entire designated Caribbean Basin area has become an integral part of the military and security system of the United States. This integration is central to Washington's strategy for dealing with political instability in the neocolonial zones.

The economic, geopolitical, and military-strategic mechanisms of the CBI have been legitimized through ideological and programmatic acceptance by the U.S. state, the multilateral lending and development institutions (such as the International Monetary Fund), the private sector transnationals, and the capitalist-dominated regimes in the Caribbean. In an important sense the CBI is designed to produce a new status quo in which the private sector will be stronger, the state will be weaker, and the masses will be pushed several steps farther away from achieving the self-determination that was promised them by the present rulers of popular anticolonial struggles. In spite of, and largely because of, their exclusion from state power the masses have been left with certain basic beliefs and convictions: (1) they have a basic right to control power as the deprived majority in societies where race, wealth, and power are still positively correlated; (2) the government is accountable to the governed; and (3) democratic freedoms of speech, organization, association, and protest are theirs by right (these being a part of the legacy of the Westminster tradition). Commitment to these beliefs is influenced or constrained by other factors such as small size of the economies, absence of abundant natural resources, international interdependence, the necessity for foreign investment, the cultural primacy of religion, and so forth. The perceptions, motives, and behavior of individuals, groups, and classes are significantly affected by these factors in existential terms.

Although the traditional plantation/commercial ruling class had been dislodged from direct control over the state (Munroe 1972), it maintained its economic position and increasingly came to share economic power and extract surplus value with foreign capital and the new "state" class—the petite bourgeoisie. The economic ruling class is still very visible in the directorate of the postcolonial state through its membership on numerous state regulatory agencies and boards. For example, studies by Parris (1981) on Trinidad/Tobago and Jones (1981) on Jamaica confirm this point. The state became the main instrument by which the petite bourgeoisie could extract surplus value for public and personal accumulation.

This ruling class emerged within largely backward economic formations and out of an existence based upon separation from private property and capital: In other words, this class rose to state power as a nonpropertied class. In order to accumulate capital it allied itself with local capital and imperialism and attempted to coopt and neutralize the masses. This explains why this ruling class could not and will not share power with the workers and peasants and why its natural allies have been agrocommercial capital and imperialism. Thus, whenever the neocolonial model of accumulation is passing through a traumatic stage, the petite bourgeoisie is forced to strengthen the repressive apparatus of the state in order to maintain or increase the rate of exploitation of labor power, to keep the investment climate safe, and to shore up ruling class interests as well as those of imperialism.

U.S. imperialism is most at issue here, although the role of Canada and other western countries should also be considered. In the context of geopolitical, strategic, and military factors—the so-called national security interests—and economic and commercial considerations in which U.S. general interests are expressed in the Caribbean Basin, several important issues arise: (1) the geographical proximity of these countries to the United States; (2) the definition of the Caribbean as a zone of crisis located within the U.S. national security sphere; (3) the general acceptance by all existing Commonwealth Caribbean regimes of Washington's definition of the region; (4) the perception and the acceptance of Washington's ability to promote and "protect" its interests; and (5) the general convergence of the interests of the Commonwealth Caribbean ruling classes with the interests of imperialism.

The Making of the Authoritarian State
in the Commonwealth Caribbean

Thomas (1984:37-45) traced the origins of the postcolonial authoritarian state to the colonial period. For example, he argued that the foundations of the authoritarian state were strengthened by postwar colonial policies that preserved the interests of imperialism as a dominant force in the colonies. This preservation was accomplished by protecting plantation (export) interests; keeping workers and peasants tied to the agricultural export system; adopting and implementing industrialization strategies that reinforced the inherited patterns of the international division of labor; and influencing the emergence and selection of political elites who accepted these arrangements. The role of the state as sponsor and manager of the capitalist development strategy, the integration of labor and the labor movement into the strategy through the two-party system and the trade unions, and the cultivation of a social climate favorable to the development of smooth labor-management relations also contributed to this phenomenon. Thomas argued that the failure of the workers and peasants to assume control of the state meant that several other struggles still had to be won, and these struggles had to be carried into the postcolonial period:

This would include struggles against the colonial... division of labor and its emphasis on primary... production; export specialization; minimal industrial development; against forced trade and financial links with the metropole designed to reproduce the world market internally... against foreign personnel filling crucial executive/management positions in the upper echelons of the state and the private sector; and against the limited autonomy of all local economic, political and social institutions. These aspects of the colonial state together with those established in earlier periods form the kernel out of which the postcolonial state developed (Thomas 1984:44-45).

Among the modest achievements of the postcolonial state, as seen by Thomas (1984:50-56), are the following: the broadening and the diversification of foreign relations; the expansion of the state into the rural economy; the fostering of the neocolonial strategy of industrialization; the broadening of the proletariat and the increase in the extent of class formation; the development of the bureaucracy; the creation of national institutions in economics, politics, and culture; and the rapid increase in the control exercised by the state over national life. In societies such as Trinidad/Tobago and Guyana the state has also achieved large-scale ownership of capital. The postcolonial state in the Commonwealth Caribbean has been essentially expansionist and interventionist. The mode of production, the role of agrocommercial capital, the impact of Keynesian and post-Keynesian "development" ideology, and the accumulation requirements of the petite bourgeoisie have been central to this process—that is, "the continued domination of the working people in postcolonial societies" (Thomas 1984:54).

The central question that arises at this time is: What makes the postcolonial state an authoritarian state? The authoritarian state is not to be confused or equated with tyrannical methods of rule alone, for no state is reducible to its method of rule. The authoritarian state "is a social category and is located in the specific historical and structural context of the reproduction of the material basis of life in peripheral capitalist societies" (Thomas 1984:83).

This means that the authoritarian state has to be conceptualized against the background of the mode of production and the social formation as a whole. Due consideration has to be given to the forms and composition of capital and the class elements associated therewith. Capital presupposes labor and therefore the wage labor-capital relation, the development/underdevelopment of the productive forces, and the ability/inability to reproduce labor power and value are important to the state which must try to guarantee these processes. The nature, aspirations, and practices of the petite bourgeoisie are reflected in the extent of market relations, social democratic norms, the impacts of the crisis of accumulation upon the class struggle, and in the relative growth of state property. The growth of the coercive apparatus of the state, as it struggles to maintain acceptable rates and levels of accumulation, mirrors its demonstrated inability to resolve fundamental problems associated with chronic unemployment, inflation, declining production and consumption, shortages of capital and consumer goods, and foreign indebtedness that exceeds the Gross National Product (GNP); and the periodic attacks by the class struggle upon capitalist accumulation.

Therefore, an examination of the material and social basis of the authoritarian state led by the petite bourgeoisie suggests that social reproduction in such an environment requires the exercise of greater degrees of control over the workers and peasants. Thomas details the problem in the following terms:

> Given all this, the ability to maintain existing patterns of internal domination rests heavily on the ability of the state to win a reduction in the growth of real wages and the standard of living of the masses, along with increased worker productivity. Without these there can be no lasting increase in the profitability of the state and the private sectors.... It is out of the effort to ensure increased profits and reduced share of wages that the state is forced to restructure, and it is out of this process that an authoritarian state emerges.... The crisis of society and the world economy together engender a crisis that threatens the continuation of the regime... as well as the continued social and economic domination of the class and state on whose behalf it rules. It is because of this that the authoritarian state is a specific product of a conjuncture of world capitalism and peripheral capitalist development. Its imposition is the ruling class response to the crisis confronting the society. *Its persistence and security are impossible without the material and ideological support of imperialism* [emphasis added] (Thomas 1984:88).

Clearly, the authoritarian state is a social-historical product with a more or less specific gestation period. It is bound up with the attack of the class struggle upon capital accumulation and imperialist hegemony.

Imperialism and the Authoritarian State

The Cuban Revolution, the crisis in the Dominican Republic in 1965, the black power revolt in the English-speaking Caribbean in the 1970s, the radicalization process in the Commonwealth Caribbean as reflected in the anti-imperialist policies of regimes headed by the late Forbes Burnham, Michael Manley, and the late Maurice Bishop, and the victories of the national liberation revolutions in Central America (among other factors) have forced the United States to define the Caribbean as a zone of crisis. For a while, Burnham, Manley, and Bishop seemed neither to accept nor to accommodate their regimes to the U.S. definition of the Caribbean. The links among Guyana, Grenada, Jamaica, Cuba, Nicaragua, and the liberation movement in El Salvador led the United States to restrict the freedom of independent action open to these and all other regimes in the region. The United States saw Cuba as the head of a strategy to weaken U.S. influence and jeopardize declared U.S. security interests in the region.

Jimmy Carter began the move in the direction of declaring the Caribbean a zone of crisis (Watson 1982a). Thus, domestic and foreign policies and actions of Caribbean regimes have come under broader and more intense scrutiny by the United States. The definition of U.S. national security interests has therefore been broadened. The legal-juridical definition and scope of the national sovereignty of Caribbean states have been further compromised. The United States is prepared more than ever before to determine the outcome of regime selection and succession in the region. It does not matter whether the political systems are based upon two-party competition, one-party government, or the absence of political parties and elections. What is important (in the U.S. schema) is that these regimes demobilize the left, strengthen military and security forces, and adopt strategies that are "realistic." Realistic strategies include those that broaden the role of the private sector, control the working class, reduce the role of the state in the economy, and provide U.S. imperialism with free and equal access to resources and economy (Watson 1984c). The Reagan administration has declared that neither "nutmegs" nor "bananas" are at stake in the Caribbean Basin; rather, U.S. national security is at stake.

Prior to the Cuban Revolution the United States had carried out at least forty-seven military interventions against Central America and the Caribbean countries. Thirty-eight of these interventions had been carried out before the Bolshevik Revolution. Therefore, communism has not been a sufficient condition to stimulate U.S. imperialism's expansionist drive (Mark 1983:16). The anticommunist response by the United States to revolutionary upsurge in the Caribbean Basin strengthens the foundations of the authoritarian capitalist state.

Imperialism is not, however, the sole contributor to the development of the authoritarian state. So far, I have traced the postcolonial authoritarian state in the Commonwealth Caribbean to a set of social conditions rooted in the Caribbean social formations and in the present conditions of imperialism. But as I noted before, there is a symbiotic relationship between these authoritarian states and imperialism, given the extent of imperialism's involvement in the region and the requirements of capital and petite bourgeois class power and rule.[4]

It is clear, therefore, that the transformation of the Caribbean into a zone of military conflict has included the rapid and unprecedented growth of U.S. military presence in the area. For example, the U.S. naval facilities at Key West, Florida have been renovated to serve as the headquarters for the commander of U.S. Naval Forces operating in the Caribbean Basin and the Pacific Ocean bordering on Central America. Other U.S. naval military facilities are located in Bermuda, Andros Island (Bahamas), Guantánomo Bay (Cuba), Antigua, the Canal Zone, and Roosevelt Roads (Puerto Rico), which is one of the largest naval installations in the world and serves as the locus of the Caribbean and South Atlantic naval command.

Imperialism plays a major role in boosting the self-confidence of the ruling class in the authoritarian state. Imperialism performs this function by strengthening its presence and providing military and related technical assistance, including training for the military and the police. Some basic features of this process in the Caribbean include the development of the Rapid Deployment Force and the Caribbean Task Force at Key West, the increase in the number of military maneuvers, the rise in the level of military aid, and the increase in the number of visits to the Caribbean by U.S. Defense Department officials. Ocean Venture '81 was indeed "the most massive maneuver since the Second World War" (Beruff 1983:18).

The rapid expansion in U.S. military sales and security assistance to the region is a concrete example of the increase in the level of U.S. preoccupation with security in the Caribbean. It is also clear evidence that the military and the police apparatus of the Caribbean state is being firmly integrated into the U.S. military and security machine. The susceptibility of these instruments of state power to the objectives of U.S. imperialism, which do not exclude repressive action against local populations, should not be underestimated. I will return to this theme later. Clearly, the Reagan administration has emphasized military and security aspects of state power and the containment of Cuba and the national liberation movements in the region while significantly downplaying economic assistance. According to the State Department:

> In the... Caribbean region, we find a growing challenge to emerging democratization from insurgency and terrorism encouraged and supported from outside the region and through proxies. Thus, our efforts, while remaining... economic, must nevertheless include military resources adequate to provide a shield behind which the processes of democratization and the reestablishment of economic stability and ultimately growth can continue (U.S. Department of State 1984:5).

A basic ideological tenet (and myth) that justifies the militaristic and interventionist policy of the United States in the Caribbean Basin asserts that there is a convergence of U.S. ideals and strategic interests and that whatever threatens democracy and "democratization" threatens U.S. security interests. Thus, working class struggles against exploitation, political repression, and the ravages of foreign capital and backward domestic capital are, by definition, threats to U.S. security interests in the Caribbean (Watson 1984c:3, 20). Any form of cooperation between a given Caribbean country and Cuba, for example, is perceived as a security problem for that Caribbean country and, by extension, for the United States (Lewis 1982:8).

Ruling classes in the Commonwealth Caribbean are caught in a set of contradictions from which they see no escape apart from closer ties with the United States. This means greater economic exploitation and stronger repression for the workers and peasants and a wider leverage for imperialism. Yet the promise these ruling classes made to the masses—"that they could and would provide [them] with the economic [and political] inheritance from which they had been... deprived by colonialism and the local landed [and commercial] oligarchy which dominated the economic system"—cannot be fulfilled under these terms (Lewis 1982:8). Once again the link between the domestic and external determinants of the authoritarian state become obvious.

Manifestations of Authoritarian State Power in the Commonwealth Caribbean

The essence of the state is not reducible to the patterns of its rule. The basic function of the state is to guarantee the set of economic, political, technical, ideological, and security conditions that are required for the reproduction of the social formation. The capitalist state in the Commonwealth Caribbean has to face these responsibilities. In the face of protracted economic crisis and political instability, and as a result of the failure of the petite bourgeoisie to keep its promise to workers and peasants, the ruling class has moved itself and the state closer to imperialism. In this respect a social psychology of weakness and dependence that is a product of class interests has forced the ruling class to "develop policies of seeking to derive resources on the basis of proven allegiance [to U.S. imperialism]" (Lewis 1982:50).

In essence these measures are a part of what the neocolonial ruling class considers necessary to do when it rules (Therborn 1980). The late prime minister of Barbados, Tom Adams, argued that U.S. "military assistance should be regarded as a watershed in the region in that, for the first time, such assistance was sought from within the region rather than from outside" (Diederich 1982:10). Tom Adams' right to speak for the population of Barbados derived not only from the ruling class assertion of a "right" to speak for all classes in society but also from the confluence of the following related conditions and circumstances: (1) the weakness of local political and economic institutions forces this ruling class to build closer ties with "the international structures of domination"; (2) the class project of the petite bourgeoisie requires the systematic weakening, neutralization, and destruction of any independent institutions of the exploited classes; (3) thus, neither independent working class political parties, organs of communication, nor free and independent trade unions have blossomed in the Commonwealth Caribbean; and (4) the absence of a revolutionary national liberation tradition in the Commonwealth Caribbean is in large measure a product of the socialization and historical development of the people of these countries. These conditions and circumstances have strengthened the position of the authoritarian state vis-a-vis the society.

In addition, the colonial and postcolonial history of Caribbean peoples has been shaped by exposures to imperialist cultural values at home and abroad. Although many Caribbean people may not support military intervention or the increasingly authoritarian character of the state, they are not necessarily disposed to adopt a critical attitude toward these forms of domination or penetration; nor are they disposed to anti-U.S. or anti-British sentiment because in many ways they are and have viewed themselves as products of the "British system." Until now most people in the Commonwealth Caribbean have not viewed the United States as an imperialist power because they had not confronted directly the naked force of U.S. imperialism. These masses still view the United States as a land of opportunity to which relatives migrate and then send back money.

In many ways Commonwealth Caribbean societies identify with the material values of U.S. capitalism. Several fundamentalist religious organizations in the Caribbean have traditions that are rooted in the values of their U.S. counterparts. Anticommunism, which underscores the religious ties and the political, military, and economic alliances between Caribbean regimes and the United States, finds widespread support at the popular level. There have been few ideological referents outside of the colonial-imperial value system. Thus, U.S. influence may be more widespread at the ideological-cultural level than is generally assumed.

Migration and other forms of economic and cultural penetration of Commonwealth Caribbean national life by imperialist forces have profoundly influenced the self-concepts of these populations. Thus, many Grenadians assumed that the invasion of their country by the United States would mean easy emigration to the United States and perhaps a new status for them, such as that which is enjoyed by Puerto Ricans. West Indian masses have, as a result of their exclusion from power, considered emigration to be the one reliable way to escape poverty and make a life for themselves. This aspect of migration has had a profound impact upon the formation of the working class and the reproduction of labor power and value and has given the ruling class an excessive degree of leverage in dealing with the masses. Migration, a phenomenon of world capitalism, has fundamentally internationalized the Caribbean working classes. The fluidity of significant sections of the working classes has had, and continues to have, major consequences for the structure of the working class, its organization, its forms of consciousness, and for the class struggle.

In addition, the fact that the Commonwealth Caribbean masses have been largely excluded from state power means that they have not really shared in the benefits of democracy in any significant ways. This raises an extremely important question: Namely, how susceptible are people who have not experienced democratic norms and culture to the imposition of authoritarian state power? In the case of Guyana, Burnham was able to impose the authoritarian state in spite of, and partly as a result of, the upsurge in the class struggle since the 1970s. The law, the constitution, and the judiciary were manipulated in "constitutionalist" and pseudolegalistic ways to achieve these ends (*Day Clean* 1980).

In Grenada, Eric Gairy arbitrarily monopolized power, used "his" parliamentary majority to enact legislative abuses, and created a paramilitary terroristic gang (based upon personal loyalty) to reinforce his rule. Although the masses did not simply accept these impositions, neither the Guyanese nor the Grenadian situation witnessed the rise of an armed, revolutionary, national liberation movement to put an alternative program on the agenda. The point is that, invariably, these societies are susceptible to the consolidation of the authoritarian state, the roots of which are traceable to the colonial past. During the crisis that led to the implosion of the Grenada Revolution, Maurice Bishop was accused by some party members of wanting to impose a "one-man rule" of Gairy vintage. His critics within the New Jewel Movement (NJM) insisted that they would fight against his rule just as they had fought against Gairyism. During the protests and demonstrations against the detention of Bishop by the Central Committee of the NJM, Bernard Coard is reported to have declared that the masses could protest and march as much and as long as they liked because they had protested and marched until they got tired during the Gairy period. In Coard's view, apparently, they could do the same under the People's Revolutionary Government (PRG) because he was convinced that they would go home when they were tired of protesting and marching (Watson 1984a).

Coard seemed to believe that although the masses had a democratic right to freedom of expression and organization as well as a right to demonstrate against the regime's practices they were not necessarily entitled to the redress of their grievances. Of course, protest by the citizenry in capitalist democracies does not presuppose that the state will accede to their demands either. In the case of Commonwealth Caribbean neocolonies where no single class has been able to establish a clear hegemony over the state and where the petite bourgeoisie's first priority is self-perpetuation, it is to be expected that mechanisms of repression will come to play a much greater role in the maintenance of the status quo. The fact that the Commonwealth Caribbean working classes have been largely unable to reproduce themselves (because of the nature of local capitalism) has rendered their existence rather precarious. This reality, plus the manipulations of the petite bourgeoisie, has fundamentally precluded the emergence and the survival of independent working-class institutions. Because the working class is fractured, it lacks organizational strength to mount an independent and class-conscious struggle against the bourgeoisie and imperialism. As such, the working class is still very much "a class in itself." This factor is of great significance in any explanation of the susceptibility of the working class to bourgeois influences and authoritarian state practices.

The workers' movement in advanced capitalist countries has not demonstrated any sustained commitment to the goals of socialism/communism. Perry Anderson (1977) argued that Western Marxism is "a theory without a practice." In the Third World the National Liberation Revolution (NLR) is still basically nationalist, fundamentalist, and revolutionary democratic. Marx's insistence that the contradictions in capitalism must develop before the system can be overthrown means that the productive forces must be developed on the basis of the expansion and maturation of the proletariat. The question of delinking based upon backwardness of the productive forces derives from the thesis of revolutionary rupture at the weakest link in the chain. The NLR has been faced with the herculean task of modernizing productive forces, rationalizing capital accumulation, and establishing democratic norms along revolutionary lines. But these projects have generally been sabotaged by the local capitalists, some sections of the working class and the peasantry, and imperialism. Socialism is not reducible to economic redistribution based upon backwardness and political repression. In the Commonwealth Caribbean, Michael Manley, Maurice Bishop, and Forbes Burnham, respectively, labeled their systems democratic socialist, noncapitalist, and cooperative socialist. However, the rule of capital remained dominant in each of these systems even where the economic and political role of the state was considerably increased.

Thus, a deep-seated economic crisis, political instability, and the weakness of existing national institutions together with the class project of the petite bourgeoisie strengthen the potential for the consolidation of the conditions on which the authoritarian state can thrive. The ruling class identifies the state with society.

The state is represented as the chief unifying force and symbol in society. It is perceived to stand above racial, ethnic, religious, and class differences. Development problems are defined in terms of resource base, economic scale, technology, legal and administrative capabilities, capital shortages, and other technical requirements, all of which are perceived in largely idealist and neutralist terms. Thus, class, power, exploitation, and domination are excluded from any definition of the problem. Anyone who questions the status quo is seen as an ideologue and a potential subversive according to this positivistic ideology.

The implosion of the Grenada Revolution has served to bolster the confidence of the petite bourgeoisie and to make its class project appear more appealing and palatable to the masses.[5] This has two effects. It provides a justification for increasing and strengthening the role of the military and the police in the national life of these societies, and it gives U.S. imperialism a golden opportunity to facilitate this process while simultaneously integrating local military and police instruments into the U.S. system. In an important sense the Grenada crisis and the subsequent U.S. invasion meant the "end of West Indian innocence." Gordon Lewis observed that "the long term lesson of Grenada is that we can no longer hold to the traditional definition of the Caribbean; it is inexorably linked to Central America" (quoted in Diederich 1984:10). As in Latin America, Commonwealth Caribbean leaders now share the view common in Washington: Well-armed and well-trained armies are the only security they have against left-wing "subversion" (revolutionary upheavals).

The signatories to the regional security pact of 1982 agreed to extend the system beyond Barbados, St. Lucia, Antigua, St. Vincent, and Dominica to include St. Kitts-Nevis "and to invite Grenada after it has an elected government." Montserrat, Anguilla, and the British Virgin Islands have also been encouraged to join (Diederich 1984:11). National security is the theme of this new regional security strategy. Barbados serves as headquarters and its government currently pays 49 percent, or $240,000, of the cost with the other signatories contributing 51 percent based on an assessment of $35,000 per country (Diederich 1984:11). Barbados has a tremendous advantage over the other signatories with its higher standard of living, an expanding defense force, a large per capita national military expenditure, and a high military outlay per soldier. The other signatories do not have armies. They rely on the local police to provide security. In the event of a "crisis," they are to contribute troops as need arises. This means that they will have to militarize their police forces, a step that is already being taken. According to Diederich (1984:11):

> The smell of cordite hardly had time to dissipate in Grenada when special forces training teams from Fort Bragg, North Carolina, began landing on neighboring islands with new weaponry.

The late prime minister of Barbados, Tom Adams, was an ardent supporter of the regional security force concept and program. He made this clear in a speech delivered to the Forty-Fifth Annual Conference of the Barbados Labour Party on January 21, 1984:

> An element of land forces should be included in the two year old regional security pact.... A study is now under way to determine whether we can establish a full regional defense force thus extending the protection available against necessary adventures, other external aggression, domestic revolution or other violent episodes. My feeling is that one regional army rather than a number of national armies would give us an additional safeguard, namely the protection of small governments against their own armed forces (quoted in Diederich 1984:10).

Adams contended that existing governments need to be protected against their own armies and populations. A regional army would protect each government from its army and people because national armies can no longer be trusted to protect a given regime. Adams advocated a regional approach to security and repression. Given the fact that the Commonwealth Caribbean countries lack the professional, technical, and financial resources to train, organize, and deploy such a regional defense force, this plan would push them further into the arms of the United States "for weapons and training and that throws us more under the U.S. military establishment" (statement by Errol Barrow quoted in Diederich 1984:11).

There is a U.S. special forces training team on each island. Each team consists of eight men, except for St. Vincent and the Grenadines where there is a six-man team and Jamaica, which has a twelve-man team. At least twenty-five men are located at the headquarters team. Training sessions last for six weeks and "include becoming familiar with the new weapons, learning to shoot straight with the ammunition, map reading and basic military field operations and procedures" (Diederich 1984:11). The graduates from the program are to replace the so-called Caribbean peacekeeping force that followed the United States into Grenada. Those who have been stationed in Grenada have also received this training. All of the newly trained troops are to operate "under one command and would move into any island which shows signs of revolutionary crisis" (Diederich 1984:11). The passing of Tom Adams may lead to a weakening of the zeal for this regional security approach, but the overall concept may still receive support from the United States.

In the absence of regular armies, the police forces in the Eastern Caribbean countries are being reorganized and equipped to engage in military activities. Each police force is to develop "a special service unit (SSU) equivalent to the American SWAT teams to function as paramilitary units" (Diederich 1984:12). Because U.S. law prohibits aid to foreign police forces, the assistance Washington is providing to these police forces has to be classified as military assistance. The regional defense strategy and the militarization of the local police are necessary to protect both the local ruling classes and the interests of U.S. imperialism. This strategy will reduce the need for future direct military invasions and occupation by U.S. forces. The Eastern Caribbean regimes are now full-scale proxies of the United States in its own "backyard."

These developments have clear and ominous implications. Reactions to the ongoing consolidation of the authoritarian state as signified by this militarization have been coming from opposition parties. James Mitchell, leader of the opposition in St. Vincent and the Grenadines, who readily supported the invasion of Grenada, argued that his country does not need to be militarized. He preferred technology and jobs whose purpose is to make the working class productive and facilitate the reproduction of labor power and value (Diederich 1984:11). St. Lucia's opposition declared that Prime Minister John Compton, in

> turning his hand at helping the United States to virtually subjugate these islands... is busy reducing the area to U.S. satellite status and this necessitates a firm military presence in all the islands of the Eastern Caribbean. The whole thrust and attitude of the police force has changed overnight. The skills of criminal investigative work and good police methods have all been swamped by the new militaristic thrust. Now our special service units strut and swagger around Castries with automatic weapons in their hands.... This cannot be good for the state especially as a number of raw recruits have come into the force at the

deep end and have plunged into techniques of killing before they have learned the responsibility of policemen and the sanctity of life (quoted in Diederich 1984:12).

The government of John Compton replied that national police forces have to be trained in countersubversion in order to become a part of the Caribbean peacekeeping force. The Green Berets from Fort Bragg now will be able to pass on their experiences from Southeast Asia and Latin America to the police forces in the Eastern Caribbean.

The party system, the electoral system, the trade union movement, and the relationship between government and opposition are unlikely to be the same again. The allocation of the national budget among different programs such as health, education, welfare, agriculture, and the military has also begun to change. The military and the police are destined to become key competitors in the battle for limited financial and technical resources. The military and security forces are acquiring a new sense of strength, ideological self-confidence, and a clear technological advantage, all of which emanate from their ostensible function as "savior of the democratic system."

The U.S. government is doing everything possible to bolster the position of the military and the police in the Eastern Caribbean. Under the fiscal year 1985 bilateral assistance program requests for Central America and the Caribbean, the Reagan administration anticipated providing the Eastern Caribbean (excluding Guyana and Trinidad/Tobago) with $57.3 million to be allocated under the Economic Support Fund (ESF), which includes military assistance, the International Military Education and Training (IMET) program, the Military Assistance Program (MAP), and the Concessional Foreign Military Sales Loans (Watson 1984c:38). Jamaica was to receive $103.25 million, with $75.25 million falling under these same military and related programs. In 1978, Barbados ranked 130 among the world's countries in terms of public expenditure per soldier. The outlay was $1000 per soldier. By 1980, Barbados' rank had risen to 70, and its expenditure per soldier had increased 900 percent to $9000. Total Barbadian military expenditure was $1 million in 1978 compared with $9 million in 1980, or 1.1 percent of the GNP. Jamaica was spending 0.08 percent and Trinidad/Tobago was spending 0.03 percent of the GNP on the military in 1980 (Watson 1984c:36).

Danns (1984:11) has shown that in 1984 the Guyanese state was spending 10.06 percent of the national budget on the military compared with a combined outlay of 9.8 percent for health and education and 7.7 percent for agriculture. The 1984 military budget of Guyana amounted to $41.03 million and was distributed as follows: Guyana Defense Force, $18.10 million; Guyana Police Force, $9.87 million; Guyana National Service, $7.67 million; and Guyana National Guard, $3.02 million. In 1966, at independence, there were 2,631 security forces in two units in Guyana. In 1984 there were 17,708 security forces in five units (Danns 1984:9-10). Guyana represents the paramount militarized authoritarian state in the Commonwealth Caribbean in terms of the ratio of military personnel to civilians and the number and range of military institutions. Burnham had called on the military to declare itself "personally loyal to him/the party and its policies and the government" in the name of "socialism" (Danns 1984:36-37).

Although the features of militarization are not identical in each and every country, common patterns are emerging. Throughout the region the military and security apparatus is expanding through increased financial outlays for military purchases, training, and military, technical, and material assistance. Increased militarization also is a result, both direct and indirect, of a production crisis, declining standards of living, and uncontrollable foreign debt. Repression is on the increase, and the security forces are being increasingly politicized. This is destined to have profound consequences for the professional status of the "security force" of these societies. The creation of the regional "security force" is designed to coerce the masses into submission and to dissuade them from any political and social action that may be useful in their struggle against exploitation and repression. Security forces are instruments of state power.

Governments are increasingly relying on the use of violence executed by gangs against the opposition, such as has become a common feature in Jamaica. The National Service, the Guyana People's Militia, and the army and police collectively carry out action against striking workers in Guyana while Parliament and the courts are used to demobilize the working class in its struggle against state capitalist repression. Electoral and legal processes are being consistently manipulated to serve the objectives of these regimes, most of which have lost genuine popular support and now rely on creating their own "mass" base to legitimize their unpopular rule. Anticommunism and national security doctrines are the foremost weapons in the ideological arsenal of these regimes.

The military is rapidly developing new political attitudes toward the masses. Alienation is on the increase in the ranks of the military. Concepts of family and community solidarity are being increasingly eroded. The military is now providing the recruit with employment, livelihood, and a sense of worth and pride where hopelessness and despair existed before. Loyalty to the army and to the state is bound to increase where the professional and highly politicized soldier is considered the keeper of the peace, the protector of order. If Washington succeeds in restricting the role of the state in the economy as proposed under the Caribbean Basin Initiative, this will have disastrous consequences for the existing weak institutions both in the state and in the society. Such an eventuality could strengthen the military and security apparatus, dramatically alter the balance of social forces, and increase the role of U.S. imperialism as a bargaining force in regional politics.

Conclusion

The rapid expansion and the growing visibility of the military and security instruments of state power in the national life of Commonwealth Caribbean societies are directly related to the protracted economic and political crisis in the region. Preoccupation with the myth that Commonwealth Caribbean political systems are by nature and persuasion democratic has reinformed related beliefs both at the state and societal level. This project has raised several important issues about the nature of the state in Commonwealth Caribbean society. To recapitulate: The state in the Commonwealth Caribbean has been developing a distinctive authoritarian nature and character in the postcolonial period, a character traceable to colonialism, and this authoritarian state has evolved along constitutionalist lines as in Guyana. The tendency to equate the substantive elements of state power and practice with constitutional provisions adds to the confusion about the nature of the state and serves as a convenient ideological instrument in the hands of the ruling classes and their supporters.

Traditionally, because of the absence of a strong military and corporatist presence, the Commonwealth Caribbean state has been considered part of the Westminster democratic tradition. The petite bourgeoisie that exercises state power has systematically employed populist-nationalist strategies of cooptation, neutralization, and control to rally working class support for the ruling-class "project." As the general economic and political crisis has deepened and as the economic and national security interests of the petite bourgeoisie and of imperialism have come under attack, the populist strategies have been found increasingly inadequate to shore up the ideological base of the system.

In these circumstances, frantic measures have been taken to strengthen the military and police, as was reflected in Jamaica, Trinidad/Tobago, and Guyana in the late 1960s and particularly during the 1970s. Simultaneously, these regimes adopted openly antiworking-class policies. The adoption of legislation such as the Industrial Relations Act (1970) in Trinidad and the Labor Relations and Industrial Disputes Act (1974) in Jamaica and the systematic employment by the state of military and paramilitary instruments to break working-class resistance in Guyana are among the foremost illustrations. These measures have been integrated with other policies to create a new populist and corporatist bureaucratic compact consisting of the state (as government), management (capital), and labor. These measures cannot resolve the contradictions that are reproduced by neocolonial accumulation strategies because the problems lie in the nature and processes of neocolonial capitalism. In some instances the state also acts as capitalist (as in Guyana) where it "commands" the economy. Essentially, the workers and peasants are still awaiting the delivery of their birthright (i.e. access to property, jobs, a decent standard of living, and democratic politics) and they recognize that economic wealth, dominance, and power are exercised by the local agrocommercial interests, the petite bourgeoisie, and foreign capital. They also recognize that this alliance of interests is the major impediment to their self-actualization. Thus, labor remains unruly no matter which political party is in power and in spite of the evident alliance of the government, opposition and the agrocommercial interests.

The expansion of the state has witnessed a deepening process of bureaucratization that has further removed the popular masses from any control over the state and also has reduced the direct accountability of the petite bourgeoisie. Populism, corporatism, and bureaucratism have therefore assumed greater importance in the face of the growing working class struggles and the deepening of the accumulation crisis. In economic terms the workers and peasants are challenging the status quo because they are finding it increasingly difficult to maintain their own economic and social reproduction and improve the conditions of their material culture. The upshot of all these developments, as I have indicated, is that the military and the police are now being fully integrated into the political mediation process as decisive and highly politicized bargaining agents. It is possible that this may give rise to what Lewis (1982) called the "coup countercoup" syndrome, but such an eventuality will depend upon the balance of class forces and how the class struggle confronts the existing model of accumulation, imperialism, and the class project of the petite bourgeoisie.

The authoritarian state does not necessarily assume identical forms at all historical junctures. The late Tom Adams, the architect of the regional defense strategy, had anticipated both the class struggle and the potential for military intervention that come with the new emphasis upon the politicization of national security and the military in these societies. He welcomed the regional pact of mutual assistance as the answer to domestic revolutionary upsurge against existing regimes. The Eastern Caribbean ruling classes believe that they have found the answer to their inability to overcome the contradictions of neocolonialism: a permanent repressive apparatus that exists for the purpose of preempting and liquidating revolutionary upheavals, and protecting capitalism and imperialism. If anything, this new development confirms that the Commonwealth Caribbean state is in desperate straits and, like a drowning man, is grasping at anything it thinks can save it. Thus, the state's authoritarian nature is now laid bare for all to see.

Notes

As elsewhere in this book, all monetary amounts are expressed in U.S. dollars in order to make comparisons easy.

1. For details of the debate on the postcolonial state, see, among other works, Alavi (1972); Boron (1979); Goulbourne (1979); Leys (1976); Saul (1974); Thomas (1984); Watson (1984a); and Ziedman and Lanzendorfer (1981). More general treatment of the state in advanced capitalist countries includes the thesis of instrumentalism represented by Miliband (1969, 1983). Poulantzas (1976) represents the "relative autonomy" thesis. Other discussions of this capitalist state are to be found in Althusser (1971); Blanke, Jurgens, and Kastendiek (1978); Gold (1975); and Jessop (1977, 1982). Jessop (1977) discusses the debate about state monopoly capitalism that is part of the thesis on the state held by some of the so-called Eurocommunist parties.

2. Aglietta (1980) discusses the question of crisis as a form of "rupture" as applied to the advanced capitalist formations. Regarding the Third World, practically every title on underdevelopment speaks of the crisis of neocolonial accumulation. There is little doubt that the thesis of a crisis of neocolonial accumulation is influenced by the dependency/world systems analysis. Implicit in this analysis is the idea of an ideal capitalist accumulation model

represented by the United States and Western Europe. The U.S. model is contrasted with underdevelopment, which is said to be reproduced in the Third World and to prevent capital accumulation and development. This perspective is considerably influenced by the ideology of economic nationalism and positivism. For a critique of this perspective, see Watson (1984c).

3. First and foremost the state is an instrument of class rule, and this is at the heart of the existence of the class struggle under capitalism. But the class struggle is a process with more or less economic, political, and ideological manifestations. Therefore, to speak of an authoritarian state is not to reduce it to the political exercise of power in society. The alignment of class forces in society, the extent to which this alignment produces and reproduces class fractions and/or coalitions around the state, and the hegemony of an individual class affect and mediate the class struggle in profound ways.

In the case of the Commonwealth Caribbean there is no doubt whatsoever that the local capitalist class exercises its direct economic dominance over the means of production and capital accumulation. Where the state owns the essential means of production and operates the economy according to capitalist rationality, the results are not very different for the working class. These capitalists also strengthen their political and policy influence through, among other methods, (1) membership on policymaking governmental statutory boards; (2) parliamentary representation; (3) economic organizations that exclusively represent capitalist interests; and (4) direct representation in public enterprises.

In essence, then, the identification of the state in terms of its authoritarian political features must also include the economic orientation of the economically dominant interests as well as the development orientation of the political forces that directly exercise political power—for example, petite bourgeoisie. Thus, although it may seem that the definition of the authoritarian state is "productionist" on the one hand and "coercionist" on the other, these elements have a legitimate place in the conceptualization of the capitalist state in the Commonwealth Caribbean. To the extent that "politics is the concentrated expression of economics," the authoritarian state is the concentrated expression of economic crisis, political instability, backward capitalism, and exclusion of the masses from state power. How else can the state in such conditions guarantee systemic reproduction except through an authoritarianism secreted underneath the formal constitutional mechanisms and technical instrumentalities of bourgeois norms?

4. Thus, it is clear that all those measures to which the post-colonial authoritarian state and imperialism are now resorting to in the name of security, stability, economic development, and democracy (the Caribbean Basin Initiative) are intended to safeguard capitalism in the region. Issues such as restructuring, counterrevolution, opposition to national liberation movements, and militarization are the necessary expression of this phenomenon.

5. The petite bourgeoisie is clear about the need for foreign capital and private capital as a whole to develop the productive forces. This class does not see any options outside of capitalism, even though it may be prepared "to toy" with notions of revolutionary democracy. However, when the class struggle attempts to push the system beyond these limits and attacks capitalist accumulation, the petite bourgeoisie finds no alternative but to strengthen the foundations of the authoritarian state. Thus, the authoritarian state is also a product of the direction of the class struggle found in these countries. As such, the authoritarian state is not an anomaly or a deformation. It is the distinct product of capitalism in the periphery where the forces of national liberation and socialism come into conflict with the forces that must uphold class society and private property. Only the development of the proletariat and its independent institutions can make socialism possible. It seems, then, given the prevailing reality, that the days of capitalism in the Caribbean may be far from being numbered.

3

The Increasing Emphasis on Security and Defense in the Eastern Caribbean

Dion E. Phillips

The Caribbean is presently the arena of international competition for power and influence over the microstates of the region, including those of the Eastern Caribbean.[1] The traditional view that the subregion comprises only client states is an artifact of the past. Rather, in the aftermath of decolonization from Britain, the prevailing situation in the Caribbean is conditioned by complexity and fluidity. These former colonies of European powers are caught in the web of the attempted reassertion of U.S. hegemony; the ideological challenge of Cuba; the ambitions of the so-called middle powers in Latin America (Venezuela and Mexico); and the behavior of other Caribbean nation-states. These interlocking factors combine to form a theatre of conflict in the subregion. Hence, the current crisis in Caribbean international relations and economy is a product of the transition of the region from an old international colonial order to a new order whose configuration is yet to be determined, despite the reversal of the Grenada Revolution.[2]

This chapter examines the relationship between the international crisis in which the Caribbean is enmeshed and the increasing emphasis on security and defense matters in the microstates of the Eastern Caribbean (see Figure 1). Specifically, this chapter shows how the U.S. and the Caribbean governments' perception of the crisis in the region as well as the former's attempt to reassert its hegemony in the world are directly related to the increased emphasis on security. This chapter also underscores the events in the late 1960s and after that predispose Eastern Caribbean countries to adopt the security model, a decision that constitutes a coincidence of interest between U.S. and local elites.

The key to understanding the increasing emphasis by the U.S. and some Caribbean governments on security lies in grasping the exigencies of the current international crisis. The prevailing international crisis in the Caribbean ensued as a result of the development impasse that confronted the region at the end of the 1960s and continued throughout the 1970s. Initially, the problem was

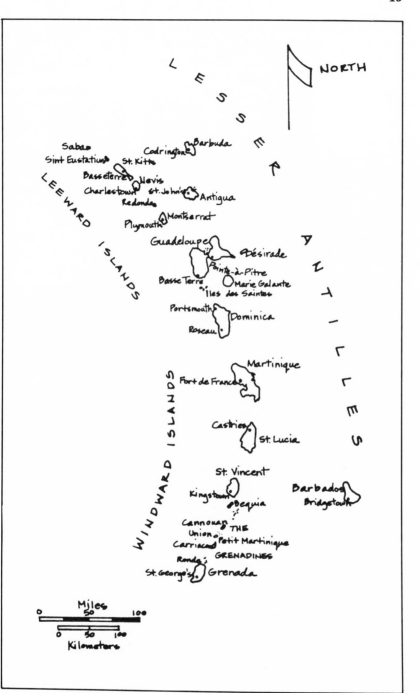

conceptualized as one in which the countries of the region were experiencing "growth without development" and in some instances little or no growth at all (Watson 1975). In the late 1970s this critical situation was compounded by a sharp increase in oil prices. As Caribbean economies attempted to cope with this debilitating, critical condition, familiar patterns of politics were being eroded in one microstate after another to the point where the region was considered by the United States as unstable.

Between 1962 and 1983 the English-speaking Caribbean experienced two waves of independence. The contemporary wave of independence began when Jamaica and Trinidad/Tobago won their independence from Britain in 1962. A second wave of decolonization from Britain followed: The Bahamas achieved independence in 1973 and Belize in 1981; all six islands of the Eastern Caribbean that had been Associated States gained their independence (St. Kitts/Nevis is the most recent).[3]

This gradual withdrawal of Britain from the Caribbean and the political and economic instability the withdrawal left behind were interpreted by U.S. policymakers under the Carter administration's second phase (1979) and under Reagan, his successor, as a strategic vacuum in the Caribbean area. It was felt that such a vacuum was unsettling to the balance of power between the East and the West and thus raised fears that Cuba might exploit the situation to extend its influence. Hence, at the Pentagon, there emerged a new comprehensive strategic vision (of the Caribbean) that integrated regional issues within a larger global framework.[4]

Emergence of the Security Model

There are specific political events that occurred in and outside of the Eastern Caribbean in the late 1960s and through to the 1980s that have progressively influenced the adoption of the security model. Beginning in the late 1960s the left in the Caribbean mounted a challenge to the postindependent status quo under the banner of black power. In 1968 Jamaica was shaken by riots as a consequence of which Guyanese historian, the late Walter Rodney, a vocal advocate of social change in his capacity as a University of the West Indies lecturer, was declared a persona non grata by the Jamaica government. In 1970 the February Revolution in Trinidad came perilously close to unseating the Eric Williams government. Moreover, in many of the Eastern Caribbean countries, a number of loosely organized pressure groups sprang up out of disaffection with the governing elite. Many of these radical groups caused area governments great concern and would in later years pose a greater threat when they adopted a more well-articulated socialist and nationalist profile.

These developments, coupled with threats to several regimes in the Eastern Caribbean, were unsettling. But the real catalyst to the militarization of the Eastern Caribbean was, however, the coming to power of the Bishop regime in Grenada in March 1979 and extraregional events such as the Nicaraguan Revolution in July of that year. Likewise, disturbing events in Afghanistan and Iran and Cuba's decision to dispatch troops to crush a Somali invasion that threatened the socialist regime in Ethiopia added to the catalysis.

Barbados

Barbados moved to formal independence in 1966 under the leadership of Errol Barrow who, although a nationalist, did not require that the U.S. Naval Facility in the northern parish of St. Lucy be removed.[5] In 1975 Barbados witnessed its first brief encounter with cold war politics in the postindependent period: In sympathy with African liberation movements, Barrow and the ruling Democratic Labour Party (DLP) gave Cuban aircraft bound for Angola permission to refuel in Barbados until Washington expressed its displeasure at the practice.[6] Mindful of the dependent nature of the Barbados tourist-oriented economy on the U.S., Barrow was constrained to comply.

However, the globalization of the conflict in the Eastern Caribbean subregion and the concomitant highlighting of the need for security were ushered in with the Cubana Airline tragedy on October 6, 1976, off Barbados. A Cubana Airline DC-8 turboprop on a scheduled flight from Guyana to Havana via Trinidad, Barbados, and Jamaica crashed in the sea approximately ten minutes after departure from the Grantley Adams International Airport (then called Seawell) in Barbados. All seventy-three passengers and five crew members were killed. This air disaster and other related events occurred at a time when the four Caribbean Commonwealth countries of Jamaica, Trinidad/Tobago, Barbados, and Guyana had opened diplomatic relations with Cuba (in October 1972).[7] Responsibility for the tragedy was subsequently claimed by anti-Cuban exiles stationed in Venezuela.

Even prior to the Cubana air disaster, Prime Minister Tom Adams of Barbados surprised the Caribbean on October 1, 1976, when he declared that two U.S. nationals were involved in a conspiracy designed to topple his two-month-old government. Adams claimed that such a conspiracy involved John Bank and Sidney Burnett-Alleyne (the latter allegedly a member of ex-Prime Minister Errol Barrow's Democratic Labour Party) who together with 260 men were scheduled to overthrow the Barbadian government after having landed at Bottom Bay, St. Philip.[8] The prospect of that experience forced the ruling Barbados Labour Party (BLP) to change its 1976 manifesto position on defense and security.

The position of Adams and the BLP in the September 2, 1976 general election had read: "The party will not commit our country to any foreign defense pacts. Internally, the defense forces will be limited to such as are adequate to maintain law and order. There will be no need to maintain any standing army" (BLP Manifesto 1976:15). However, as a result of the Burnett-Alleyne plot, the BLP then took the converse view in its 1981 General Election Manifesto—namely, that "events within Barbados, the Caribbean and elsewhere, have proved the need for Barbados to have a limited Defense Force with a capacity to withstand the immediate assault of potential marauders, terrorists and mercenaries" (BLP Manifesto 1981:13).

Such acts of aggression as have occurred in Barbados, coupled with other developments in the region and in the world generally, have had an overriding effect on the current regional preoccupation with security and defense.

Grenada

After 1951 politics in Grenada was dominated by Eric Gairy; despite his domination, Gairy proved increasingly inept as a leader in the years following Grenada's independence in 1974. Gairy's Grenada United Labour Party (GULP) had two sets of opponents. On one side was Herbert Blaize's Grenada National Party (GNP) and the Committee of 22, whose members were drawn from the Chamber of Commerce, the Rotary and Lions clubs, the established churches, and organized labor. The GNP's election record against Gairy was feeble, and the alliance was too sober to attempt removing Gairy by force. That alternative fell to the second opposition group, a small party called the New Jewel Movement (NJM) led by Maurice Bishop. Because of the corrupt nature of the electoral process and Gairy's repressive measures—which were mainly carried out by the Mongoose Gang, a group of hired thugs—the traditional avenues to social change were blocked, and hence violent revolution seemed the only alternative. Accordingly, in the predawn of March 13, 1979, NJM activists seized Gairy's True

Blue barracks while he was in the United States, and within an hour his government was toppled.

Almost a month passed after the takeover before Frank Ortiz, Bridgetown-based U.S. ambassador to Barbados and the Eastern Caribbean, paid his first visit to Grenada. Even though the Gairy administration had left behind intractable economic problems, the United States offered the Grenadians a meager $5,000 in aid. Moreover, Ortiz informed Bishop that the United States "would view with displeasure any tendency on the part of Grenada to develop closer ties with Cuba." Bishop would later respond on April 13th during a radio broadcast by stating: "No country has the right to tell us what to do or how to run our country or who to be friendly with. We are not in anybodies (*sic*) backyard" (Marcus and Taber 1983:30-31).

These strident remarks were operationalized three days later when Grenada's People's Revolutionary Government (PRG) opened formal diplomatic relations with Cuba. This action predictably alarmed conservative opinion in the neighboring Eastern Caribbean and in Washington and set in motion a course of events that would later fuel the argument in favor of greater security both inside Grenada and in the neighboring Eastern Caribbean states.

Gairy's sordid politics did not endear him to fellow Caribbean heads of state, most of whom silently approved his overthrow. These leaders developed a modus vivendi with Bishop. However, many were reluctant to fully embrace the PRG because of its method of attaining power and its reluctance to hold elections.[9] Naturally, the PRG, isolated and surrounded by apparently unfriendly neighbors, identified Cuba and other countries of that political orientation as its allies. As Grenada's dependence on aid from nonaligned and socialist countries such as Algeria, Iraq, Libya, and Syria grew, this reinforced its proclivity to adopt "principled positions" on sensitive foreign policy issues. This stance included supporting the Soviet Union in U.N. votes on Afghanistan and offering to send 500 Grenadian troops to fight in Namibia in May 1980 (Gill 1981).

Dominica

Despite the objections of opposition leaders, Dominica became independent in November 1978 under the leadership of Patrick John. Shortly thereafter, the John regime, no longer constrained by its semicolonial status, enacted new laws restricting freedom of the press and banning civil servants and other workers in essential services from engaging in strikes. The stalemate came to a head in June 1979 when armed forces opened fire and killed three protestors during a demonstration in the capital city of Roseau. Dominicans reponded to this occurrence by calling a general strike and forming the Committee for National Salvation (CNS), which was composed of business, church, and trade union leaders as well as members of opposition political parties on both sides of the political spectrum, all of whom called for John's resignation. In spite of the disintegration of the John government and widespread Dominican disfavor with his oppressive rule, he managed to hold onto power a bit longer before being forced to leave office as a result of the widespread opposition to his administration. An interim government was formed quickly under the leadership of Oliver Seraphine, John's former agriculture minister.

Although the new Dominican government comprised politicians of both the right and the left, such a coalition was labeled "left of center" because it included "Rosie" Roosevelt Douglas and Atherton Martin, well-known Caribbean leftists.[10] Before long, the Seraphine government was replaced by Eugenia Charles and the Dominica Freedom Party. In April 1981, however, there was an attempted coup against the Charles regime. Its perpetrators were a band of North American mercenaries belonging to neo-Nazi groups and the Ku Klux Klan who conspired to overthrow the government of Dominica and reinstate the pro-South African regime of ex-Prime Minister John.

On December 19, 1981, there was a third coup attempt involving former members of the disbanded Dominica Defense Force who launched a coordinated attack on the island's police headquarters and prison. It stands to reason, given these coup attempts in Dominica, that the U.S. decision to reassert its hegemony in the region, with a greater emphasis on security, would find a responsive chord in the Dominican government. It is therefore not surprising that Prime Minister Charles played such a visible and vital role in the joint U.S.-Caribbean invasion of Grenada.

St. Lucia

The microstate of St. Lucia gained independence in 1979 and was ruled by the right-of-center prime minister John Compton. Since 1972 the social inequalities engendered by the economic policies of the Compton regime have led to widespread dissatisfaction. Compton has responded to this discontent by passing a harsh Public Order Act and cracking down on protest by unemployed youth. This act was largely responsible for the landslide victory of the St. Lucia Labour Party (SLP) over Compton's United Workers' Party in the July 1979 general elections. The SLP remained in power until 1982 when it fell to the pro-U.S. United Workers' Party. The SLP included such leftist leaders as George Odlum (who became the deputy prime minister) and Peter Josie. Odlum, who was thought likely to be the next prime minister of St. Lucia, publicly supported the NJM regime and there were reports that Grenada was giving St. Lucians military training (Gill 1981).

The victory of the SLP was interpreted, both in and outside the Caribbean, to mean that the microstates of the Eastern Caribbean were moving sharply to the left. Such a deduction was further reinforced when within a week after the election victory, Prime Minister Allan Louisy, Odlum and Josie (all three from St. Lucia) and Seraphine and leftist Martin of Dominica met with Bishop and other members of the Grenada People's Revolutionary Government (PRG) in a "minisummit" in Grenada, July 13-16, 1979. The Declaration of St. George's that emanated from the meeting was leftist.[11] Moreover, it was reported that placards were displayed at the conference that ominously sounded the political death knell of Milton Cato's rightist government in St. Vincent where left-wing forces were mobilizing and gathering support for their cause.

Other Eastern Caribbean States

In other Eastern Caribbean countries a similar wave of radicalization was in effect. Many radical groups began to test their political strength, although subsequent events in the subregion indicate that Washington's fear that "there would be one, two or three Grenadas down there before we know it" never materialized, leaving Grenada somewhat isolated in this area (*Miami Herald* 1979).

In Antigua a small but vocal party, the Antigua-Caribbean Liberation Movement (ACLM) under the leadership of Tim Hector, caught the attention of the region. The ACLM's rise to prominence grew from its exposure of the corruption of the ruling Antigua Labor Party (under Vere Bird) by means of the ACLM's newspaper, *The Outlet*. Bird's adventures included hosting the Canadian Space Research Corporation, which supplied weapons to South African forces for use in Namibia and Angola, and accommodating a U.S. "secret" underwater listening post at the U.S. naval base (*Caribbean Contact* 1980:7).

In the St. Vincent election of December 1979, the anticommunist campaign of the St. Vincent Labour Party (SVLP) gave it a resounding victory. However, unlike previous years, the left won an encouraging 15 percent of the vote. Even in Montserrat a leftist group emerged. It seemed for a time as if the political atmosphere in the Caribbean would accommodate further moves to the left—a fear proven false by a conservative backlash in the ensuing years.[12] Nonetheless, it was as a consequence of this short-lived political ferment in the Eastern Caribbean that the United States and conservative governments in the region viewed the interest in ideological pluralism and diversified foreign relations as a U.S. national security problem. This redefinition of U.S. policy was in vivid contrast to the days when Terrance Todman, President Carter's secretary of state for inter-American affairs, affirmed that "we no longer see the Caribbean in quite the same stark military context" (Pearce 1981:152).

Adoption of the Security Model

The failure of the economic strategies of the 1960s has resulted in a slowly developing crisis of economic and social disorganization. This disorganizaton in the Eastern Caribbean breeds resistance movements as Eastern Caribbean people seek alternative ways of transforming their poor socioeconomic condition. However, the indigenous political developments that spring from the economic crisis are perceived by U.S. policymakers and local elites as an assault on the status quo. This scenario is articulated as the spread of Soviet/Cuban ideology into a weak area, and hence is proffered as a threat (Lewis 1982:7).

The ongoing struggle of left-leaning forces in the region and the accumulation of arms in Grenada under the Bishop regime have been interpreted by U.S. and Caribbean ruling classes and the media as a security threat. Thus, Grenada's decision to arm itself was not seen as a mechanism to serve the defense of the English-speaking Caribbean's first socialist-oriented regime, which had experienced repeated threats to its authority.[13] Instead, it was perceived as an offensive in the ultimate spread of an "alien" ideology to the neighboring Caribbean islands.

As a consequence of this bipolar, cold-war view of the world, U.S. policymakers in concert with many Caribbean leaders decided to increase their emphasis on security and defense matters. Such an emphasis was concretized by four principal developments:

1. The Carter administration established a Caribbean Joint Task Force at Key West, Florida on October 1, 1979. Under Reagan, this contingency force was incorporated into

the newly constituted U.S. Forces Caribbean Command, one of three full-scale North Atlantic Treaty Organization (NATO) Atlantic commands.

2. The governments of Antigua, Barbados, St. Kitts/Nevis, and St. Lucia agreed to engage in joint coast guard patrols beginning in 1979 because of random invasion scares to many of these microstates. This loosely knit collective security agreement was institutionalized on October 30, 1982, in Roseau, Dominica when the governments of Antigua/Barbuda, Barbados, Dominica, St. Lucia, and St. Vincent/Grenadines signed a memorandum of understanding that created the Regional Security System (RSS).

3. The Organization of Eastern Caribbean States (OECS) as well as Barbados and Jamaica permitted the use of their forces to assist the United States in the Grenada invasion and to serve on the multinational Caribbean Peacekeeping Force (CPF) on Grenada.

4. A new wave of repression has been instituted in the Eastern Caribbean. This phenomenon is reflected in the tendency for governments in the subregion to selectively repress left-wing forces in the name of security. In 1980 the work permit of Ralph Gonsalves, a Vincentian-born lecturer at the University of the West Indies was revoked on the grounds that he had become "a security risk." Likewise, Guyanese-born Ricky Singh, editor of *Caribbean Contact*, a regional newspaper with headquarters in Barbados, lost his work permit because of his editorial opposition to U.S. action in Grenada. Also, the lyric versions of "Boots," "One Day Coming Soon," and other tunes of the calypsonian Gabby that are critical of the security mind-set of the late Tom Adams administration have been banned from the airwaves of radio stations in Barbados. Moreover, as early as May 21, 1981, the Adams government introduced into Parliament an Emergency Powers Act to forestall possible "aberrant behavior"; only public opposition stopped the legislation from becoming law. Also, the Charles government in Dominica enacted draconian security measures into law—namely, the Prevention of Terrorism Act and a State Security Act.

This expanded emphasis on security and its redefinition to include internal security grow out of the belief that Third World countries, including those in the Eastern Caribbean, are incapable of immediate and substantive economic transformation and stability. Hence, it becomes necessary to reinforce the security system of these countries as a prerequisite to eventual economic development. However, the security systems of the region are not likely to serve as a concomitant of peace for progress and development. Rather, the increasing emphasis on security and defense has the effect of serving as a prophylactic against social change and hence as the agent of crisis management, as indeed was the case in the Grenada tragedy in October 1983.

Pre-Grenada Invasion Period

The "takeoff" in the current preoccupation with security and defense in the Eastern Caribbean and in the larger Caribbean is probably traceable to October 1, 1979, when the Carter administration, on the pretext that Cuba harbored a brigade of 2,600 Soviet combat troops, established a new Caribbean Joint Task Force with headquarters at Key West, Florida. This permanent, full-time task force is equipped with a squadron of A-4 attack bombers and a radar-jamming navy electronic warfare squadron. Under the auspices of this task force, electronic surveillance and monitoring of Cuban and Soviet movements in the region were stepped up as U.S. naval exercises were expanded (Lowenthal 1984:184).

Also in 1979 the United States, in a show of power, dispatched a task force of more than fifteen hundred marines to the U.S. complex at Guantánamo Bay, Cuba to engage in military maneuvers. The sending of troops to Cuba in this manner was testimony that the political pendulum had swung away from the earlier Carter administration trend toward possible normalization of U.S.-Cuba relations. Such action in the late 1970s undoubtedly ushered in the second cold-war period in the Caribbean (Halliday 1983). Unlike the previous Carter posture, conflict and instability in the Caribbean were now perceived in East-West, rather than North-South, terms.

Another manifestation of the growing emphasis on security and defense in the Eastern Caribbean was the decision of the governments of St. Lucia, St. Vincent, and Barbados, at the bidding of the late Tom Adams, to form a pact to engage in joint coast guard patrols. This initiative in collective security was prompted by a coup threat in Dominica and another mercenary "invasion scare" in Barbados in January 1979. Also, on May 5, 1979, on the heels of the NJM coming to power in Grenada, the Antigua government claimed that it had uncovered a plot to overthrow its elected government, which involved Kendrick Radix, the then attorney general of the two-month-old PRG (*San Juan Star*, May 5, 1979:11).

As a consequence of these events in the Eastern Caribbean, the United States collaborated closely with Britain to promote the idea of collective security. Prime Minister James Callaghan of Britain agreed to provide coast guard training and support for Barbados in order to "knit together" the forces of the neighboring countries. Since 1980 Barbados and the OECS countries have ordered armed patrol boats from Britain (Adams 1982:11). The objective behind such assistance is to supplement the Eastern Caribbean islands' limited security forces. None of this assistance was earmarked for the PRG in Grenada. The United States and Britain refused to sell arms to Grenada because of their concern for alleged human rights violations and because the PRG refused to call elections. However, the United States not only provided the other Eastern Caribbean countries with security assistance, but resumed arms sales to the military dictatorship of Chile in July 1980.

During a visit to the Caribbean in August 1980, Lord Owen Carrington, then British foreign secretary, stated that "the policy generally on arms sales is that each case is decided upon its merits. Broadly speaking, we sell arms to our friends and to those whom we wish to encourage to defend themselves" (Pearce 1981:155).

However, even before Lord Carrington's arrival in the Eastern Caribbean, impetus was given to the regional security project when Barbados helped St. Vincent quell a rebellion of Rastafarian militants on Union Island in December 1979. Tom Adams clearly welcomed the role of subregional police and offered to send troops to any island that requested them. With this "sweet success," Barbados' security posture in the Eastern Caribbean was consolidated; Barbados became the pact's headquarters, and Colonel Rudyard Lewis, chief of staff of the Barbados Defense Force, served as the pact's commander.

Ever since the emergence of the Bishop regime in Grenada, the United States and many of the governments of the Eastern Caribbean have been known to attach increasing importance to security matters as an alleged democratic protective shield against "alien" ideology. With the election of the Reagan administration to office and the arrival of the "hawks" in the Pentagon, there was a predictable change in U.S.-Caribbean military policy. According to Joint Chief of Staff David C. Jones, the Caribbean was "becoming part of a comprehensive strategic vision that integrated regional issues within the larger global framework" (Tiryabian 1984:49).

Unlike Latin America and Haiti, the military was not a major actor in the English-speaking Caribbean. Until the United States and its allies built a modest indigenous military capacity in the islands of the Caribbean, where little or none previously existed, the United States resorted to an enhancement of its own military presence in the waters of the Caribbean. Ocean Venture, which featured a full-scale dress rehearsal of the invasion of Grenada on the Puerto Rican island of Vieques during August-October, 1981, was the largest peace-time naval maneuver since World War II.

Additionally, in November 1981 the U.S. Defense Department reorganized and upgraded its regional defense network under a single umbrella—U.S. Forces Caribbean Command—and granted the command new status as one of the three full-scale NATO Atlantic Commands. As a concomitant of the creation of this new command, the navy shifted most of its routine Atlantic Fleet training to the Caribbean. This new command's area of responsibility comprises the "waters and islands of the Caribbean, Gulf of Mexico and parts of the Pacific bordering Central America" (Tiryabian 1984:49). It encompasses the Caribbean Joint Task Force, which Carter established at Key West in 1979, and the Antilles Defense Command in Puerto Rico as well as naval forces and air force, army, and marine units.[14]

Not only did the Reagan administration step up its military presence in the Caribbean as expressed in the frequent staging of naval exercises but the actions of selected Caribbean leaders converged with those of the Reagan administration. On October 30, 1982, a memorandum of understanding was signed in Roseau, Dominica by the governments of Antigua/Barbuda, Barbados, Dominica, St. Lucia, and St. Vincent/Grenadines. This event, which inaugurated the Eastern Caribbean Regional Security System (RSS), constituted the widening and institutionalization of a defense and security pact involving the coast guard forces of Barbados and select OECS countries that was agreed upon in 1979 soon after the PRG came to power in Grenada. The document was signed in the company of Rudyard Lewis, chief of staff of the Barbados Defense Force, as well as Orville Durant, then deputy commissioner of police in Barbados (*Caribbean Contact* 1982:16). The main objective of the RSS is to coordinate the multiple security systems in the Eastern Caribbean by means of an international organization.[15] The government in Barbados is mainly responsible for the creation and shaping of this joint police and military cooperation, and it contributes 49 percent toward a central fund with the remainder being shared equally among the other participating countries.

As part of the security role carried out by the Regional Defense Pact in its formative years, and also as further evidence of the augmentation of security considerations in the Eastern Caribbean, a small security team was installed in the U.S. embassy in Bridgetown, Barbados, and Antigua was chosen as the site for the Barbados embassy's first branch office in the region and hence as an additional base for intelligence activities. Also in 1980, the U.S. government's Voice of America radio station set up a relay transmitter on the island of Antigua to broadcast especially to the Eastern Caribbean.[16] Clearly, the adoption of the security model as the appropriate manner in which to address social change and instability in the Eastern Caribbean has gained significant momentum and acceptance in the subregion.

The acid test of this manifest commitment toward a greater emphasis on the use of security in the Eastern Caribbean was the assassination of Maurice Bishop and the events that followed. Prior to the tragedy the hostility toward the Bishop regime by the right-wing governments of the Eastern Caribbean and Barbados and by the Reagan administration was no secret. For most of Bishop's tenure in office, these countries adamantly opposed the NJM's style and policies and systematically harassed Bishop and his colleagues.[17] Although the Reagan administration, and, to a lesser extent, the conservative governments of the region might have wanted to take direct action to undermine the Bishop regime, the appropriate opportunity had not yet presented itself. However, the larger significance of the assassination of Prime Minister Bishop and the outrage this action provoked provided member states of the OECS, Barbados, Jamaica, and the Reagan administration, in particular, the opportunity they had long been awaiting.

The Reagan administration's decision to invade Grenada was made in light of Reagan's reelection campaign strategy. Reagan was mindful of the condition that precluded Carter's reelection—namely, that revolutionary students had seized nearly one hundred U.S. citizens and held them captive in the U.S. embassy in Teheran, Iran. Moreover, the Russians had invaded Afghanistan, a South Korean airline had been shot down, and the Beirut bombings had cost the lives of more than two hundred U.S. citizens. Hence, a get-tough policy by the Reagan administration was politically expedient and consonant with the U.S. desire to reassert its hegemony in the world. Grenada, a small country in the Eastern Caribbean located in what the United States regards as its "sphere of influence," was a tailor-made medium through which the United States could flex its political muscle.

Not only did the leaders of the membership countries of the OECS, Barbados, and Jamaica issue a formal request for the U.S. intervention in Grenada, but the United States was nominally supported in its October 25, 1983, invasion of Grenada by a token force of soldiers and police from four of the OECS states—Antigua/Barbuda, Dominica, St. Lucia, and St. Vincent—as well as Barbados and Jamaica. Such a decision was a manifestation of the deepening attachment of Eastern Caribbean countries to the security model. The Grenada invasion was a resounding reminder to the Caribbean and the world that, unlike the post-Vietnam era, the United States was again prepared to invade sovereign countries, if need be, as a sign of its geopolitical strength. The Eastern Caribbean had become a military arena of world renown, a fact that would inescapably heighten the emphasis on security in the subregion.

Post-Grenada Invasion Period: Militarization of the Police

The U.S.-led invasion of Grenada in October 1983 was a military success for the United States and served to reinforce the perceived need for authentic security in the Eastern Caribbean. Concretely, the realization of this need has taken the form of the militarization of the police in the Eastern Caribbean. This tendency is a reflection of the Reagan administration's foreign policy, which is inextricably linked to its military policy. Hence, the use of force in Grenada and the military success that ensued seemed to confirm the usefulness of the security model.

On November 7, 1983, one month after the Grenada invasion, a bipartisan U.S. congressional delegation led by Thomas Foley visited Grenada to investigate the advisability of the Reagan administration's decision to send U.S. forces to Grenada. On leaving Grenada, the Foley delegation met with the heads of government of the Organization of Eastern Caribbean States and Barbados at Sam Lord's Castle in Barbados, at which time a request for U.S. assistance in training regional military and security personnel was made. A separate request was also made by the sitting chairperson of the OECS, Eugenia Charles, for the revitalization of a "proper" police force in Grenada. This initiative for the further embracing of the security model in the Eastern Caribbean came as no surprise. Both Eugenia Charles and Vere Bird, two key figures in the OECS leadership, had long since heralded the need for a greater U.S. role in Caribbean affairs. Such an orientation was received with so much popular acclaim in the subregion that even Cameron Tudor, a former deputy prime minister of the centrist DLP in Barbados, said that the U.S. naval facility in northern Barbados should never have left Barbados in 1978 (Tudor 1983).

The request for additional military assistance by Caribbean leaders was approved fifteen days after the petition was made. The Reagan administration agreed to provide a $15 million peacekeeping package for the security forces in the region.[18] Beginning in December 1983 U.S. military aircraft delivered military supplies including vehicles, weapons, and communication equipment to the security forces of Barbados, Dominica, St. Lucia, St. Vincent, and Antigua; "accelerated infantry training programs" were provided as well.

The alleged rationale behind this new regional security strategy, which involved the arming and training of police soldiers in selected Eastern Caribbean countries, is national security. However, Barbados, the headquarters of this militarization thrust, and Antigua are the only two governments in the Eastern Caribbean with standing armies. As a consequence, police forces in the countries that are signatories to the regional defense force concept are being reorganized and equipped to engage in military activity in the event of a "crisis." Each police force is involved in the process of developing a Special Service Unit (SSU). These units are equivalent to U.S. SWAT teams and are intended to function in a paramilitary capacity; the most important aspects of their training program are instruction in counterinsurgency and indoctrination of U.S. values.

Most of the graduates from these military training programs replaced members of the "multinational Caribbean peacekeeping force" in Grenada that was created in the aftermath of the U.S.-led invasion of that island. Also, many of those Caribbean security personnel who were relieved of duty in Grenada as well as some members of the newly constituted Grenada police force were recipients of this special training. These newly trained troops are being coordinated under the command of the RSS and would be able to move into any island which showed signs of revolutionary crisis. Moreover, as the first formal training program for SSUs drew to a close in September 1985, the United States indicated that it will continue to provide updated training and assistance to the region.

The Rise and Role of the Regional Security System

Three months after the Grenada tragedy in October 1983 the idea of a regional defense force as a concomitant of the arming of the police was broached. On January 22, 1984, at the forty-fifth annual conference of the ruling BLP, it was revealed by Tom Adams that the signatories to the Regional Security and Military Pact had agreed to extend membership to newly independent St. Kitts/Nevis and that Grenada would join the pact after elections were held in December 1984. Montserrat, Anguilla, and the British Virgin Islands, although crown colonies, were also encouraged to join. In terms of the future configuration of subregional security in the Eastern Caribbean, Adams declared that plans were afoot for the Regional Security Pact to be transformed into "a full regional defense force, thus extending the protection available against necessary adventures, other external aggression, domestic revolution or other violent episodes [and that]... an element of land forces should be included in the two year old regional security pact" (*The Nation* 1984:1). Adams, the architect of the new regional defense strategy, believed that "one regional army rather than a number of national armies would give us an additional safeguard, namely, the protection of small governments against their own forces" (*The Nation* 1984:1).

On February 8, 1984, U.S. Secretary of State George Shultz traveled to Central America and the Caribbean on a trip that included stops in Grenada and Barbados. The objective of this trip was to discuss, among other things, "the security of the islands." The proposal in support of a single Regional Defense Force was tabled at this meeting, but it gained U.S. support. Shultz stated, however, that the U.S. was looking carefully at the cost and logistics involved.

Also, in February 1984 a delegation from the House Armed Services Committee visited Barbados and Grenada. The delegation was briefed by Brigadier Rudyard Lewis, commander of the RSS, on the need to develop a permanent security force in the regon.[19] As shown in Table 3.1, Lewis indicated that of the 3,370 police in the Eastern Caribbean, only about 10 percent, or 360, have received any paramilitary training. Hence, he emphasized the necessity for providing military training to the seven police forces of the Eastern Caribbean in order to offset the acute shortages of regular armed forces in the region.

On March 17, 1984, the government leaders of the six Eastern Caribbean countries involved in the defense and security pact convened their second meeting in a month at the Barbados Defense

Force headquarters to finalize basic arrangements for establishing one regional defense force rather than a number of national armies. Although the United States promised it would consider the proposal for a regional defense force, such a costly venture never materialized. In lieu of the creation of a regional defense force, the United States, with support from Britain and Canada, is providing assistance and training for the modernization of Caribbean security forces under the rubric of the RSS.

Table 3.1

**Size of the Various Security Forces
In the Eastern Caribbean, 1984**

Country	Defense	Reserves	Police	Police Special Service Unit	Coast Guard
Antigua	6	0	350	55	19
Barbados	270	250	1,500	50	90
Dominica	0	0	375	80	25
Grenada	*	*	*	*	*
St. Kitts	0	0	300	30	0
St. Lucia	0	0	425	80	23
St. Vincent	0	0	420	65	25

* Grenada's security forces were disbanded after the U.S. invasion and replaced by a 350-strong multinational Caribbean Peacekeeping Force. Beginning in 1984, the United States, Britain, and Canada assisted in the training of new security forces.
Source: U.S. House of Representatives, Armed Services Committee (1984).

The U.S. role in facilitating increased defense and security in the Eastern Caribbean is irrefutable. As evidenced in Table 3.2, U.S. military assistance to the Caribbean between 1981 and 1984 has uniformly risen. In fact, during this very period most countries in the Eastern Caribbean have, for the first time, become beneficiaries of U.S. military aid. Moreover, the U.S. Congress allocated an increase in aid for 1984 and 1985.

Current U.S. military aid to the Eastern Caribbean is a watershed event in U.S.-Caribbean relations. These countries lack the professional, technical, and financial resources to modernize their

60

Table 3.2

U.S. Military Aid to the Eastern Caribbean, 1980-1984
(in thousands of $)

Country	1950-1980	1981	1982	1983	1984	Total
Antigua	0	0	0	***	***	0
Barbados	64	61	170	77	***	372
Dominica	0	12	317	***	***	329
Grenada	0	0	0	0	15,000†	15,000
St. Lucia	0	0	0	0	***	0
St.Vincent	0	0	300	***	***	300

*** Figures were not available for individual country at date of publication.

† This $15 million was given out of Peacekeeping Funds, not as DOD military aid.

Source: U.S. Department of Defense (1983).

respective security forces. However, U.S. assistance to Eastern Caribbean countries makes possible protection against social and civil upheaval. Moreover, the participation of police and soldiers from selected OECS countries, Barbados, and Jamaica in joint maneuvers with U.S. and British forces, as exemplified by Exotic Palm '85, has the effect of integrating Eastern Caribbean countries and Jamaica into the U.S. global military establishment.[20]

This being the case, certain segments of Eastern Caribbean society have exhibited "reservations" with regard to the escalating militarization of the region. Such skepticism has come from spokespersons of opposition parties. Upon coming to power in 1985 Prime Minister James Mitchell of St. Vincent echoed his government's disinclination to become involved in further militarization of the region, although as of this writing, St. Vincent remains a member of the RSS. Critics of the military build-up argue that the RSS is, at best, only able to play a limited role in regional security and that ultimately it constitutes a threat to the independence and territorial integrity of the countries of the region because the only logical role for the RSS is to take charge of internal security. Rather, opponents of Caribbean militarization support the call for the Caribbean to be declared a zone of peace.[21]

Conclusion

The tendency toward an increasing emphasis on security and defense matters in the Eastern Caribbean is not an evil in and of itself. However, the progressive expansion of security systems in the subregion is occurring at the expense of much-needed further democratization. This accelerated process of militarization in the Caribbean stems from the interpenetration of external and internal factors. Externally, the new interventionist foreign policy of the United States promotes the rise and institutionalization of a Regional Security System, part and parcel of which is a militarized police. This bolstering of "client security forces" among the new nation-states of the Eastern Caribbean is consonant with U.S. national security objectives.

Internally, Caribbean elites are known to support U.S. objectives in the subregion because they coincide with these elites' increasingly repressive stance toward their own populations. This fact is not only corroborated by the acquiescence of Eastern Caribbean leaders to unprecedented U.S. military assistance, but is also evident in the inclination of those very governments to increase budgetary state expenditures for security.

A hidden message in the promotion of this new regional defense strategy seems to be that in spite of Grenada, the United States is loathe to commit its own troops and is attempting to form a bloc of friendly Caribbean nations which will collectively be responsible for Washington's view of national and regional security in the Eastern Caribbean. Hence, the United States, with some assistance from Britain and Canada, will train, equip, and coordinate the security systems in the Eastern Caribbean. These local security establishments are expected to play the central role in keeping their societies together. In so doing, Eastern Caribbean security systems will serve as the bulwark of the status quo and as the protector of U.S. political and economic interests.

Notes

1. For purposes of this chapter, the term "Eastern Caribbean" refers to the English-speaking countries in the Eastern Caribbean: that is, Antigua/Barbuda, Barbados, Dominica, Grenada, St. Lucia, St. Vincent/Grenadines, and St. Kitts/Nevis, which are all former colonies of Britain, as well as Montserrat, Anguilla, and the British Virgin Islands.

2. The U.S.-led invasion of Grenada in October 1983 is indicative of a heightening of the international crisis in the Caribbean

62

and points to the intensity of the political conflicts that have developed in the region.

3. Jamaica and Trinidad/Tobago achieved independence in 1962; Guyana in 1964; Barbados in 1966; the Bahamas in 1973; Grenada in 1974; Dominica in 1978; St. Lucia and St. Vincent/Grenadines in 1979; Antigua/Barbuda in 1980; Belize in 1981; and St. Kitts/Nevis in 1983. Anguilla, the British Virgin Islands, and Montserrat are the only former colonial possessions in the Caribbean that remain crown colonies.

4. From 1979 to 1981 U.S. defense journals were filled with a number of articles advocating a new vision of the region; see Sims and Anderson (1980).

5. The U.S. Naval Facility, which included an underwater listening post, was removed in 1978 during the BLP administration. The facility was relocated to Antigua.

6. The Cubans were transporting troops to Angola to aid the Movimento Popular de Libertação de Angola (MPLA) in their struggle against União Nacional para a Independência Total de Angola (UNITA) and Frente Nacional de Libertação de Angola (FNLA), two rival factions that enjoyed the support of South African combat troops; see Duncan (1978).

7. Within the space of six months, anti-Castro exiles claimed responsibility for bombing the Guyana consulate in Trinidad and sabotaging a Cubana Airlines luggage cart in Jamaica and the Cubana Airlines office in Barbados.

8. In January 1979 Barbados experienced another invasion scare. Tom Adams responded by calling for joint coast guard patrols.

9. Among Caribbean leaders only Michael Manley of Jamaica and the late Forbes Burnham of Guyana actually supported the PRG. The other leaders openly opposed Grenada's socialist-oriented path to development. Even the late Eric Williams, prime minister of Trinidad/Tobago, bluntly refused to open the letters sent to him by the PRG.

10. Douglas, along with fellow leftist Agricultural Minister Martin, was dismissed from the CNS in January 1980 to allay U.S. fears (the United States, after all, had provided relief aid to Dominica as a result of hurricanes David and Frederick).

11. The twenty-point declaration announced that "the three governments... recognized that popular democracy, respect for the rights of the workers and social and economic justice for the masses must be the[ir] main objectives." It also declared support

for the New International Economic Order, endorsed "an independent and non-aligned approach to foreign policy relations with all countries," and opposed "imperialism in all its forms" (Declaration of St. George's 1979: 18, 20, 21).

12. In the 1980s there was a conservative change in the politics of the region as evidenced by the regimes of Edward Seaga in Jamaica, Tom Adams in Barbados, Eugenia Charles in Dominica, John Compton in St. Lucia, and Milton Cato in St. Vincent/Grenadines.

13. The PRG documented numerous attempts at sabotage and destabilization between 1979 and 1983. One such incident took place at Queen Park in June 1980 and almost destroyed the entire leadership.

14. The Harry Truman Annex, located at Key West, Florida (decommissioned in 1973), as well as such Puerto Rican facilities as the Roosevelt Roads naval base at Camp Santiago and the communication centers at Sabana Seca and Vieques were all spruced up to accommodate the creation of this new command.

15. The RSS has a central liaison office in Barbados where contingency plans are coordinated. The modus operandi of the RSS is that upon request for assistance from a member country, the liaison office will issue a request to other member states for a contribution from their specially trained security forces.

16. As part of its global "war of ideas and credibility" with its adversary—the Soviet Union—the United States is using the airwaves and the mass media to accelerate the Caribbean people's acceptance of U.S. values. Private-sector U.S. television programming is aired in the Caribbean and comes replete with original advertising.

17. However, shortly before the Grenada tragedy, fellow Caribbean leaders in neighboring territories, who were previously openly hostile to Grenada, no longer felt frightened for their own positions and seemed ready to work with Bishop and the PRG.

18. This $15 million came from a special "peacekeeping" account that in the past had only been used for multinational observers at trouble spots such as Cyprus, Sinai, and Lebanon.

19. See U.S. House of Representatives (1984: 1-44).

20. Both Prime Minister James Mitchell in St. Vincent/Grenadines and George Chambers in Trinidad/Tobago, whose governments are leery of the militarization of the region, sent observers to the Palm '85 maneuvers.

21. The idea of the Caribbean region as a zone of peace was given saliency in a resolution adopted at the Twelfth Plenary Session of the General Assembly of the Organization of American States at La Paz, Bolivia, October 1979. This resolution refuses to define the region as a sphere of influence for any power and supports instead ideological pluralism and peaceful coexistence.

4

Violence and Militarization in the Eastern Caribbean: Grenada

Ken I. Boodhoo

An argument could be made that the brutal murder of Prime Minister Maurice Bishop of Grenada and three of his Cabinet officials on October 19, 1983, together with the deaths of large numbers of his supporters (estimates ranged from 50 to 400 dead) was the culmination of thirty-five years of steadily increasing levels of violence within that society. Whether the subsequent (and continuing) domination and militarization of Grenada by the United States alters that trend toward violence is still to be determined.

The return of native-son Eric Gairy to relatively peaceful colonial Grenada in 1949 initiated a movement that awakened the political consciousness and expectations of the ordinary people. Gairy employed various degrees of civil disobedience and violence against the colonial authorities to gain office, and he was not beyond continuing the same tactics while in office. However, the trend toward state violence and militarization eventually hastened Gairy's downfall.

Whereas the Bishop government, which lasted from 1979 to 1983, was relatively successful in meeting many of the basic needs of the majority of the Grenadian population, the earlier employment of coercion as a method of control was continued. Violations of basic human rights were numerous during this period.

The purpose of this chapter is to analyze these thirty-five years of contemporary Grenada's history with particular emphasis upon the rise of coercion and militarization in that society. Gairy's employment of coercion is discussed first and then is followed by an appraisal of the four-year government of Maurice Bishop with regard to its achievements and its violations of basic human rights. The international determinants of the increased militarization of Grenada under Bishop are discussed: linkages with Cuba and the Soviet Union, the airport issue, and constant U.S. pressure. Finally, the chapter examines the continuing militarization of Grenada by the United States and the prospects for a peaceful, democratic, and stable Grenada and Eastern Caribbean.

Gairy's Grenada: Violence and Coercion

In Grenada the thirty-year period from 1949 to 1979 was dominated by the figure of Eric Gairy, who at the time of the 1979
coup was prime minister and leader of the Grenada United Labor
Party (GULP). Born in Grenada, Gairy migrated to Trinidad at
age twenty to seek employment in the oilfields there. He later
lived in the Dutch colony of Aruba, also working in the oil industry, and for the first time became active in labor union politics.
On returning to Grenada in 1949, he utilized his organizational
skills to develop rapidly a trade union of approximately twenty
thousand agricultural and general workers.

By the early 1950s the Grenadian colonial economy was a
classic example of a small-scale, plantation-type economic system.
This economy, based on cocoa, nutmeg and sugar, was owned by
a very small, light-skinned elite group. The peasantry eked out
a living on small plots of land or through seasonal employment
offered by the small export-oriented plantations. Until the return
of Gairy, employment in agriculture offered very low wages, as was
the situation throughout the Caribbean. With a per capita income
of about $250 and high unemployment and underemployment, the
Grenadian majority suffered serious hardships.

The politico-constitutional counterpart of this colonial economic system was a crown colony government in which power
resided in the hands of the British governor and secondarily in
the civil service. Until the granting of universal adult suffrage in
1951, the majority of the Grenadian population did not participate
in the political process.

During the first quarter of 1951, Grenada experienced the most
widespread and violent strikes the country had undergone until
that time—these were called by Gairy's trade union in support of
increased wages in the sugar industry. These strikes culminated
in the largest working-class demonstration the country ever witnessed. The British, unfortunately for them, played into Gairy's
hands by sending him to jail. As the demonstrations grew for
Gairy's release, the British governor was forced to negotiate directly with Gairy in order to return peace to the colony. Gairy at
once gained the legitimacy he had earnestly sought and the governor eventually conceded that Gairy was the leader of the country's
working class.

Gairy and his GULP won the 1951 elections, but Gairy quickly
realized the major constraints placed on his power as a consequence of the colonial constitution. Although he had obtained

some degree of authority, final decisionmaking ultimately resided with the British governor. In the 1954 elections Gairy's GULP won six of the eight seats, albeit with reduced voter support; in 1957 he lost control of the legislature by winning only two seats. The party was returned to office in the 1961 elections, but financial mismanagement and charges of corruption resulted in suspension of the constitution and a call for new elections the following year. In this election the GULP lost to the middle-class, business-oriented Grenada National Party (GNP), which went on to run the country until 1967.

A major reason for Gairy's defeat in 1962 was the fact that by that time, Grenada had begun to experience a gradual restructuring of its economy. The rise of the hotel industry, and with it increased employment opportunities in construction and transportation, was achieved at the expense of the labor force in the agricultural sector. The latter was the base of Gairy's support. While the agricultural work force dropped from 12,432 in 1946 to 8,660 in 1970, employment in the construction industry increased from 2,900 to 4,200 between 1960 and 1970 (Gill 1983:3).

Gairy always counted heavily on support from the rural population, but because some members of this population were now salaried urban workers, their class interests were thereby altered. However, after five years of GNP leadership, the elections of 1967 once again returned Gairy to office with an amended and more advanced constitution, thereby permitting him greater dominance over domestic policy.

By 1967 Gairy had emerged as an extremely controversial figure. He generated intense feelings among the populace both for and against his leadership. His appeal was grounded in a curious admixture of charisma and skillful manipulation of religious symbols (compounded by his involvement in voodoo-type worship). Eventually, his power came to depend on the emergence of the repressive arm of the state, including the ill-famed Mongoose Gang.

It was almost inevitable that Gairy would turn to state repression as an instrument of control. By the late 1960s the gradual restructuring of the economy away from its former agricultural base together with Gairy's own desire to promote the capitalist path to "development"—and subsidize his increasing acquisition of personal wealth in the form of hotels, nightclubs, and other such businesses—meant that Gairy was now the defender of a whole new set of interests. Intimidation, corruption, and repression became the means for the protection and promotion of his private and public interests.

Accompanying the increase in represssion was the steady physical deterioration of the country's basic infrastructure: the road system, medical services, and educational facilities. Allowing the educational facilities to deteriorate was deliberate on Gairy's part because ignorance was necessary in order to perpetuate the myth of his "divine mission." Further, the shift in employment to the urban sector had not only created a new working class but also encouraged thousands to flock to the capital in anticipation of sharing in the benefits of this new class. This population movement exacerbated the unemployment situation, which by the late 1960s was close to 50 percent. A climate of fear and repression among the increasingly economically depressed ordinary people in Grenada provided the setting for the rise of the New Jewel Movement (NJM).

From NJM to Coup: A Decade of Terror

By the late 1960s, the economic situation in Grenada more or less mirrored that of other English-speaking Caribbean countries. Operation Bootstrap, the Puerto Rican model of industrialization by invitation, had, through the introduction of inappropriate technologies, left a legacy throughout the region of severe unemployment and exacerbated class divisions. At the same time, free university education provided the dispossessd with opportunities hitherto reserved for the elite while young, foreign-trained graduates from largely middle-class backgrounds were returning to the region.

A convergence of economic depression and advanced education for a wider group of Caribbean society provided the impetus for the black power movement throughout the region. This movement, building on thought developed by the New World Group a decade earlier, was in the forefront of mass demonstrations, which erupted in Jamaica in 1968, moved through the chain of islands, and enveloped Trinidad in February 1970.

Passing through Trinidad at precisely that time on his return home to Grenada was Maurice Bishop. Son of a middle-class, St. George's businessman, Bishop had just completed legal training in England during which time he was also involved in West Indian minority politics. In May 1970, two months after his return to Grenada, Bishop, together with a core professional group that was later to emerge as the leadership of the NJM, participated in a mass demonstration in St. George's in sympathy with the Trinidad movement that focused attention on Grenada by demanding "more jobs now" (Jacobs and Jacobs 1980:85).

The response of the Gairy government was swift and immediate. Within ten days of this demonstration Gairy had the Emergency Powers Act approved by the legislature. This act granted the police broad powers to search private premises for "subversive literature," guns, and ammunition without first being required to obtain a warrant; the act also restricted the movement of persons, limited the right of freedom of assembly, and rationed essential services and commodities. In a speech delivered two days later, Gairy boasted:

> We are now doubling the strength of our Police Force, we are getting in almost unlimited supplies of new and modern equipment.... Opposition referred to my recruiting criminals in a reserve force. To this I shall not say yea or nay. Does it not take steel to cut steel? Indeed hundreds have come and some of the toughest and roughest roughnecks have been recruited (cited in EPICA 1982:45).

The May 1970 demonstration began a new chapter in Grenadian politics. It was the first time that Gairy and his GULP faced opposition from a group other than the middle-class GNP. This new group was beginning to appeal to the working class, the original base for Gairy's own support. To meet this challenge Gairy responded with the method he first employed while in opposition and later developed while in office: the use of force. The nurse's strike later that year provided the arena for confrontation. Gairy's forces teargassed, beat, and later arrested the demonstrators. Maurice Bishop, Kenrick Radix, and other young lawyers defended the nurses in court and gained their acquittal. This incident not only dramatized Gairy's brutality but also established Bishop, Radix, and several other young intellectuals as actors on the Grenadian political stage.

Gairy's security forces were organized into three separate branches: the army, the Mongoose Gang, and the police. After the nurses' strike, Gairy established two additional security arms: a "night ambush squad" and a "special secret police force." Once his security forces were consolidated, Gairy turned to the legislature to legitimize his repressive actions. After his overwhelming victory against the GNP in the 1972 elections, Gairy increased his personal grip and extended his repressive stranglehold over the society through the passage of several legislative acts.

In quick succession the Explosives Amendment Act (no. 4 of 1972), the Prevention of Crime and Offensive Weapons Act (no. 38 of 1972), and the Public Order Amendment Act (no. 43 of 1972) were approved in the legislature. Each of these pieces of legislation sought to restrict the freedom of the individual, give the police the right to enter and search a private home without first obtaining a warrant, and ultimately suppress the developing popular democratic movement (Jacobs and Jacobs 1980:98). Gairy's increased repression in the early 1970s encouraged the formation of the NJM.

What eventually became known as the NJM actually had its beginnings with the return of Unison Whiteman, a young economist, to Grenada in 1964. Disturbed by the conditions of the working class, he organized a small discussion group in the largely agricultural parish of St. David. In 1972 this group was formalized as the Joint Endeavor for Welfare, Education, and Liberation— JEWEL. By this time Bishop's and Radix's two-year effort against Gairy in the capital of St. George's had led to the formation of the Movement for the Assemblies of the People (MAP). The MAP opposed the existing Westminster model of government.

In 1973 the MAP and the JEWEL merged to form the New Jewel Movement. Confrontation between Gairy's forces and the NJM was immediate and violent. Within a month of the NJM's formation, following the shooting of a young man at Grenville by the police, five thousand villagers demonstrated against this unjustified killing. The airport at Pearl's, near Grenville, was shut down for three days. Later that year the NJM and the GNP were engaged in a brief alliance and called a series of worker strikes. Gairy responded with state force, which included physically abusing the strikers, jailing the leadership, and, eventually, killing a few NJM sympathizers. The events of Bloody Sunday, however, became the foremost example of state brutality and led to the coalescing of opposition against Gairy.

On Sunday, November 18, 1973, the NJM leadership was invited by a Grenville businessman to his home to finalize details for a general strike scheduled for the following day. The home was surrounded by the police, led by Inspector Innocent Belmar, who ordered the secret police to "get them dogs." Under a hail of bullets the NJM leadership was beaten, captured, dragged through the streets of Grenville, and thrown into the local jail.

The brutality of this act caused intense horror in the country and led to the formation of the nonpartisan Committee of 22—a group comprised of church representatives, business organizations, and trade unions in broad opposition to the regime—which encouraged strikes and demonstrations. But state brutality did not end. A month after the events of Bloody Sunday, Bishop's security guard was shot to death by a member of the Mongoose Gang, and just one month before the declaration of independence, in February 1974, Rupert Bishop, Maurice's father, was killed by Gairy's forces.

In Gairy's preoccupation with consolidating his personal power and wealth, he permitted the Grenadian economy to degenerate during the postindependence period. The basic infrastructure steadily deteriorated. However, the state system of repression—policemen, paid auxiliaries, soldiers, the secret police, and police stations—all expanded steadily. It was largely as a consequence of the latter situation that the overall fiscal deficit problem was exacerbated.

To compensate for the deficit, taxes were dramatically increased. By the late 1970s taxes accounted for 27 percent of Gross Domestic Product (GDP), but the deficit situation continued unabated and was one of the major causes for infrastructural deterioration.

As a consequence of the physical deterioration of the country and escalating repression by the state, Gairy's government became increasingly isolated from its regional partners in the Caribbean Community (CARICOM). At this point Gairy turned to regimes akin to his in South Korea, Chile, and Anastasio Somoza's Nicaragua. The 1977 military agreement with General Augusto Pinochet of Chile, which called for training of Grenadians in Chile and arms transfers, clearly indicated Gairy's future direction.

It was against the background of Gairyism that the NJM staged its predawn coup on March 13, 1979. The NJM later claimed that the final decision on the coup was influenced by its belief that the Gairy regime was about to assassinate the entire NJM leadership.

Grenada under the People's Revolutionary Government

Objectives and Policies

Within a few hours of the seizure of power, Maurice Bishop, leader of the People's Revolutionary Government (PRG), explained the objectives of the revolution in a radio broadcast:

> People of Grenada, this revolution is for work, for food, for decent housing and health services, and for a bright future for our children and great grandchildren. The benefits of the revolution will be given to everyone regardless of political opinion or which political party they support. Let us all unite as one (Marcus and Taber 1983:25).

Thus did the new leader outline the broad goals of his government, with an emphasis upon social and economic change for the Grenadian masses. While the emphasis was upon fulfilling the basic needs of the broad masses of the society, PRG rhetoric was nationalistic and populist in orientation. Very few could argue with the government's basic goals or even with the method of appeal. As the years progressed, however, the rhetoric of the revolution became radicalized, even Marxist-Leninist.

A fundamental objective of Bishop's Movement for the Assemblies of the People in the early 1970s, even before the establishment of the NJM, was to move Grenada away from the inherited British, Westminster form of government to the innovative Assemblies of the People. The twenty-five year rule of Eric Gairy had demonstrated that although in principle there was little fault with the British system of government, in practice parliamentary democracy in Grenada had indirectly permitted one-man authoritarian rule.

After the assumption of office the NJM established a People's Revolutionary Government as the formal seat of legislative power. Ostensibly the PRG was the provisional government, as previously outlined in the NJM's manifesto, which would ultimately give way to the National Assembly. Effective power over Grenada, nevertheless, was in the hands of the Central Committee of the NJM. The day-to-day running of the government was administered by the nine-member Political Bureau, a subset of the Central Committee. In a very practical sense final decisionmaking resided with Maurice Bishop who, from the first day of the revolution, emerged as its leader and, ultimately, the leader of the country.

It could be argued that Bishop and the NJM were attempting to create a most unique and even utopian political system, more appropriate to the scale of Grenadian society than was the West-minster system. The plan to involve much of the population in national decisionmaking was a most ambitious and difficult undertaking. Yet it may also be argued, with equal conviction, that the NJM's popular assemblies were simply one stage in moving Grenada toward the socialist model. Whereas Grenada had not yet arrived at the socialist stage—the coming into power of the working class—it could be said that the revolution was in the intermediate position, or the national democratic stage. Bishop himself stated that "we see this revolution as being in the national democratic stage. We are an anti-imperialist party and government, and we believe that the process we are involved in at this time is an anti-imperialist, national democratic, socialist-oriented stage of development" (Bishop interview, 1982*a*).

On another occasion, as Bishop sought to explain "why Grenada could not proceed straight away to the building of socialism," he emphasized:

[We] must first pass through a stage where we lay the basis... for the building of socialism. In other words, comrades, what we are now into (this national democratic stage) really means two things. What we are speaking about now is not socialist construction, not the socialist revolution, we are speaking about the national democratic revolution, we are speaking about socialist orientation (Bishop 1982*b*:3).

Bishop sought to elaborate further by contending that "national democracy" is "national because it arose from a national liberation struggle" and "democratic because it aims to give or restore rights and freedoms to the majority of the people" (Bishop 1982*b*:4).

The Economic Program

The Gairy regime left the economy in a poor condition. Major economic problems faced by the new government were negative growth rates, unemployoment running at about 45 to 50 percent, a major deficit in the country's balance of payments, and a very high rate of inflation. Bishop had repeatedly emphasized that his party's primary concern was meeting the basic needs of the majority of the society.

Thus, the goal of providing for the needs of the poorer masses coincided with the national democratic objectives espoused by the party. But again, the rhetoric of the revolution was not matched by the economic program pursued. The economic strategy pursued by the PRG was based upon the mobilization of international sources of finance in order to develop the country's resources. In order to attract funds from the international capitalist community the PRG had to temper its revolutionary zeal and create an economic climate in which these funds could be made available. Thus, the predominant role played by local and foreign capitalists was modified but not eliminated. In terms of overall economic activity the private sector continued to play the decisive role.

One of the major ironies of the NJM was that its foremost exponent of Marxist-Leninism, Bernard Coard, who served as deputy prime minister and minister of finance, was by all accounts a cautious and prudent director of the state's economic policy. For instance, whereas NJM leadership repeatedly spoke of the "movement to socialism, using the mixed-economy approach and the non-capitalist path" (Marcus and Taeber 1983:22), this was not reflected in national economic policymaking, which remained capitalistic in orientation. The NJM's respect for private property was apparent throughout its economic policies.

The government's economic policies succeeded. In a comprehensive assessment of the Grenadian economy under PRG rule, the World Bank reported that although the government had "inherited a deteriorating economy," after three years "Grenada has been one of the few countries in the Western Hemisphere that continued to experience per capita growth during 1981" (World Bank 1982). The World Bank reported that the economy grew by 2.1 percent in 1979, 3 percent in both 1980 and 1981, and 5.5 percent in 1982.

Any general assessment of the PRG's economic performance, however, must take into consideration the degree to which the national democratic objectives of the revolutionary government were fulfilled. Was the government in fact able to move the economy toward the socialist path? Most observers of Grenadian economic performance would probably say no. The PRG did very little to confront the elite landowning class: After four years the vast majority of land acreage remained in private hands. Much of the state-owned land had been inherited from the Gairy regime. State enterprises were established, but their contribution was only 25 percent of GDP. The centers of economic power in St. George's remained largely untouched. The establishment of the Marketing and National Import Board (MNIB) merely set the government in competition with the domestic capitalist class, which the government did nothing to replace. The Bishop regime appeared to do nothing more than modify and make efficient the structures of the dependent capitalist model already in place in the Grenadian economy. Despite the fact that the Bishop government instituted broad infrastructural programs to meet basic needs and reduced unemployment (at least in the short term), the economy's basic structural deficiencies were not confronted.

The Human Rights Record

Until the 1979 coup Grenada's formal political system was patterned after Britain's. Electoral politics is traditionally viewed as an important component of this system because it gives the electorate the right to effect change as it so desires. The Grenada coup was the first instance in the English-speaking Caribbean where change was achieved by nonpeaceful and nonelectoral means.

In his first official speech to the country on the morning of the coup Bishop promised that freedom of elections would be restored. A month later Bishop seemed less concerned about the immediacy and urgency of elections (Bishop interview 1979). He argued that an immediate priority was the "consolidation of the revolution." He suggested that after an enumeration of voters the country would be ready for elections. However, some four and one-half years later elections had not yet been held. By that time Bishop had taken the position that democracy was much more than "just an election"; he dismissed the idea of casting a ballot as "five second democracy" (Marcus and Taeber 1983:302). In its place he consistently promoted the notion of a participatory democracy, in accordance with his original Assemblies of the Peoples. However, by mid-1983 Bishop had announced the establishment of a constitutional commission, and it was anticipated generally that subsequent to the formulation of a new constitution elections would be held.

It is entirely possible that had the PRG government held an election that was won by the NJM, such a government would yet be running the country today. An election would have provided the NJM with the elusive legitimacy it always sought, released some of the domestic pressures for rapid solutions to domestic problems, and served to nullify some of the constant criticism from the United States and from within the region. But, fundamentally, the NJM did not encourage elections because it was unsure of their outcome. The NJM's past performance in electoral politics was only partially successful: There was always a core of Gairy supporters to be considered. The fact remains that Grenadians were not provided the opportunity to express their views on the government by electoral means. The accepted norms of behavior to which peoples of the English-speaking Caribbean states had grown accustomed were violated.

The refusal to hold elections was part of a new system of relationships enunciated by the PRG with regard to the Grenadian population. Fundamental to the new relationship was suspension of the 1974 constitution and rule by the periodic declaration of People's Laws. For instance, People's Law no. 8 provided for preventive detention without charge or trial of persons suspected of endangering public safety. By 1981 more than one hundred people had been detained under this law. By October 1983 there were seventy-eight political detainees at Richmond Hill Prison and another twenty-five members of the Rastafarian sect held at the Hope Vale detention camp. In 1983 Amnesty International itself admitted that it did not know the total number of persons being held in preventive detention (Amnesty International 1983:138).

In addition to detention without trial, there were numerous allegations of ill-treatment and even torture of political detainees. Russell Budhall and Layne Phillips, for instance, both claimed to be kicked, beaten, and burned while being held in detention (Budhall and Phillips 1983). Amnesty International sought to investigate these charges but with limited success (Amnesty International 1983:138). However, Episcopal archdeacon Charles Huggins was permitted to conduct weekly religious services at Richmond Hill, which gave him the opportunity to monitor activities there, and thrice-weekly visits were made by doctors to that prison (U.S. State Dept 1984a:569).

Although the traditional British common law system continued to be applicable for ordinary criminal offenses, the preventive detention system operated separately, thereby denying the individual the basic right to a fair, speedy, and public trial. According to a 1980 law the latter cases were periodically reviewed by a three-member detention tribunal under Bishop's supervision in his capacity as minister of interior. However, as a consequence of the irregular nature of this review process, a few people were detained without trial for almost the entire period of the PRG government.

Such were the cases of Lloyd Noel, a former NJM member, Leslie Pierre, the PRG's first acting attorney general and editor of the *Grenada Voice*, a newspaper banned by the PRG, and Tilman

Thomas, a shareholder in that newspaper. These individuals were detained when the newspaper published its first issue after the coup. Even though the paper had declared itself loyal to the revolution, it reserved the right to criticize. With the closure of the *Voice*, the *Torchlight*, and the *Catholic Focus*, freedom of the press ended, and indeed, freedom of speech was severely curtailed.

There were no direct attempts to curtail the freedom of worship, but it is clear that the PRG believed the established churches were a threat to the revolution. In a detailed secret analysis of the Grenadian church by the government, it was repeatedly stated that the churches were opposed to the government, and even gearing up for a "confrontation with the government" (Roberts 1983). Although this conclusion might have been an overstatement, it was almost inevitable that the church would be perceived as a threat to the revolution.

The attempt to consolidate the revolution domestically did not detract from the external relationships developed and pursued by the PRG. Indeed, the leadership promoted such relationships aggressively, in spite of the fact that most of these relationships served to escalate the level of tensions between Grenada and the United States. To a great extent the revolution believed that the building of national independence domestically was inextricably linked to independence in foreign policy and support from external actors.

Grenada in the International Environment

The preindependence NJM proposals for the country's participation in regional and international affairs were not unlike the program for domestic change articulated by the party after 1979. Indeed, the NJM seemed to accept the position that restructuring the society internally would require new orientations in foreign policy and in international affairs as well. It is therefore clear that the NJM was determined, from the beginning, to chart a course both domestically and internationally that would challenge the prevailing behavior of regional states, with the exception of Cuba. Moreover, such a course ultimately violated the prescriptions of the United States for the hemisphere, thereby making the prospects for confrontation with that hegemonic power almost inevitable.

Upon assuming control of the country in March 1979, the PRG faced two immediate and urgent problems arising from domestic pressures that together served to influence the state's foreign policy. The first was the fear that Gairy would seek to lead an invasion of the island and return to power. The second was the consequent need for external assistance to rebuild Grenada's economy. A call for arms to defend the state and an immediate request, too, for economic support to reconstruct the economy did not bring tangible, immediate assistance. A few countries, Jamaica and Guyana particularly, responded in accordance with their limited resources. Trinidad remained quietly hostile. Barbados, eventually, was much more openly antagonistic. Many larger countries adopted a wait-and-see attitude. The single exception was Cuba.

In April 1979 the PRG obtained its first shipment of arms from the Cuban government. Within a few months both countries approved an agreement that provided Grenada with a broad range of technical support services, training, and personnel to develop the social and economic infrastructure. This was quickly followed by the arrival of a small group of Cuban medical and dental technicians that permitted the establishment of medical services in rural Grenada.

The strengthening of the relationship between Grenada and Cuba was part of a broad pattern of new relationships in the international system never before sought by any English-speaking Eastern Caribbean state. Significant among these relationships was the immediate decision to seek entry into the Non-Aligned Movement, an entry that was in keeping with the proposals of the 1973 NJM manifesto to avoid being allied with either the East or the West. Grenada was admitted to that movement and participated in the Sixth Summit Conference held in Havana in September 1979. Grenada was later elected to the coordinating bureau of that organization.

The determination of the Grenadian government to chart an uncompromisingly independent foreign policy course, its development of close relations with Cuba and, later, the Soviet Union, its determination to establish friendly relationships with revolutionary governments, especially with Nicaragua and with Suriname, and its rhetorical war with the United States all served to exacerbate relations with the latter. Bishop nevertheless argued that the United States initiated this hostile relationship.

The U.S. Response

The English Caribbean had become accustomed to change by peaceful means. Moreover, such change, whenever it occurred, did not signal restructuring of economic or political relationships with the West. Bishop threatened these customs. Even more significantly, Caribbean states had, with the possible exception of Jamaica, maintained a policy of distancing themselves from Cuba, and this policy was still in force in the late 1970s.

On the second day of the NJM takeover, in its first meeting with U.S. representatives, the new government asked for economic assistance to rebuild the country. The U.S. consul general assured the Bishop government that he would encourage his government to provide the necessary assistance. One month later no such aid had been granted, but in the meantime two sets of circumstances laid the basis for the souring of relations between the United States and Grenada. From his base in California, Gairy repeatedly declared on radio the need for a countercoup and called for the United States to support him in this attempt. The second circumstance arose from the almost immediate offer from the Cuban government of economic and, later, security assistance.

On April 7, about three weeks after the initial takeover, a Cuban delegation arrived in Grenada to open talks on assistance programs. The U.S. government reacted with anger and changed its posture of cautious acceptance to one of confrontation. Within a few days the U.S. ambassador to the Eastern Caribbean, Frank Ortiz, arrived in Grenada and sternly lectured Bishop and his government on the hazards of establishing a working relationship with Cuba. The young revolutionary government of Grenada was incensed by the callousness of the U.S. approach. It served further to confirm the suspicions of this youthful group that the giant of the north had not eschewed a "big stick" attitude in the conduct of its foreign relations.

The U.S. government, unable to force the Grenada government to bend to U.S. will, mounted a propaganda war. The media were employed to create a picture of an increasingly repressive country becoming more steadily aligned with the Soviet Union and therefore one not safe for U.S. tourists. The State Department advised travel agencies against recommending Grenada. Grenada's alliance with the Soviet Union on the Afghanistan issue provided the United States with additional propaganda material. Further, the United States brought pressure to bear on its allies and on international lending agencies to refuse economic assistance to Grenada.

It was, however, Grenada's decision to build a new airport, and the generosity of Cuba in the building of that airport, that most dramatically escalated the level of tension between the two countries. What Grenadians saw as a powerful symbol of their resolve and determination to achieve economic development, the United States saw as a symbol of Soviet presence in the hemisphere.

Airport: Militarization or Tourism?

On March 23, 1983, President Reagan, in his nationally televised "Star Wars" speech, declared:

> On the small island of Grenada... the Cubans, with Soviet financing and backing, are in the process of building an airfield with a 10,000 foot runway. Grenada doesn't even have an air force.... More than half of all American oil imports now pass through the Caribbean.... The Soviet-Cuban militarization of Grenada... can only be seen as Soviet power projected into the region (Reagan 1983).

For six days following, various U.S. television crews sought the supposed Grenadian military base, the supposed military communication facilities, and the so-called military barracks, none of which was found.

The PRG did not initiate the idea of the airport at Point Salines; Grenadian governments since 1955 had recognized that a new airport was vital to the country's development. The present airport at Pearl's was inadequate because the runway was only 5,500 feet long; it was located between the mountain and the sea; it lacked night-landing facilities; and the drive to town was through tortuous mountains. The need for a new airport became even more apparent after a World Bank Study concluded that tourism was Grenada's main hope for financial solvency.

Some six months after obtaining power the PRG began seeking funds to build the airport. The government first approached the United States, Britain, and Canada as well as European, Arab, and Caribbean countries for assistance. Not only did the United States flatly refuse, but it brought pressure on its allies to do the same. In 1981 the European Economic Community (EEC) and Grenada organized a conference to seek cofinancing for the project. The United States again pressured its allies to stay away. Some succumbed to this pressure. Grenada's request to the International Monetary Fund for $8 million was halved in response to U.S. pressure. However, with assistance provided by Cuba, the EEC acting independently of its individual members, Libya, Algeria, Syria, Iraq, Nigeria, some Scandinavian countries, and Venezuela, airport construction began.

Most Grenadians supported the airport project enthusiastically by purchasing almost $250,000 of "airport bonds" to help finance construction. To Grenadians the airport was the major symbol of their independence and their determination to achieve economic development. President Reagan, however, saw the airport as a major propaganda weapon in his administration's war with Grenada. His government denounced the effort as an attempt by the Soviet Union and Cuba to extend their power further into the region. The Reagan administration argued that the airport would serve as a Cuban-Soviet military base, which would thereby threaten the security of the United States. Further, the State Department added that the new airport would provide a refueling stop for Cuban planes on their way to Angola and give the Soviet Union an important beachhead to control the shipping lanes through which much U.S. oil passes. Cuba, however, had been flying soldiers and supplies to Angola since 1975—obviously, then, it had resolved its refueling problems. Neither Trinidad nor Venezuela, the two countries whose shipping lanes could have been potentially affected, ever complained. In fact, neither supported the U.S. invasion. Even within the State Department itself there was skepticism concerning the administration's hysteria about the airport (Massing 1984:86-87).

Grenada, Cuba, and the USSR: The Military Connection

Under Prime Minister Gairy, Grenada had established a small army upon gaining independence. In addition to the regular police services Gairy also had organized an assortment of secret paramilitary groups, among which was the notorious Mongoose Gang and all of which were personally loyal to Gairy. The PRG dismantled the army and the secret branches, replacing them with the popular-based People's Revolutionary Army. By 1983 the army numbered close to six hundred full-time soldiers. The army was required, during conditions of peace, to be fully involved in community development projects.

In addition to the permanent army the PRG established a voluntary militia. Although at first somewhat disorganized, a bomb explosion at a public rally in June 1980, ostensibly directed at the leadership of the PRG, encouraged the government to reconstitute and reorganize the militia. Members maintained their civilian jobs, however, and received no salary for serving in the militia. They were drawn from a wide cross-section of the population and numbered between two thousand and twenty-five hundred members. There were plans to further develop the country's overall defense forces.

There is no simple answer to the obvious question: Why did the PRG consider it necessary to organize a relatively large defense force? Initially, the PRG undoubtedly was fearful that former prime minister Gairy, with some form of U.S. assistance, would lead a countercoup, and further efforts were organized within Grenada to destabilize the regime: for example, the De Raveniere Plot and the Budhall Gang (Searle 1983:39-40). The bomb explosion at the rally to celebrate Heroes Day certainly was cause for concern, and with regard to external threats, the PRG repeatedly expressed the fear of an invasion by the United States. Undoubtedly the PRG believed it was necessary to arm itself to defend the revolution.

For its part, the United States, with some support from leadership in the Eastern Caribbean, claimed that the militarization of Grenada was for the sole purpose of spreading the Grenada model into neighboring territories. Indeed, this was one of the major reasons presented by Eastern Caribbean leaders for their "invitation" to the United States to enter Grenada. To these charges Sally Shelton, former U.S. ambassador to Barbados, has responded: "I have not been convinced by the available evidence that Grenada was training West Indian leftists from neighboring islands in the subversion of democratically elected governments. The evidence presented to me had been, quite simply, very thin" (Shelton 1983:4).

As the Grenada-Cuba relationship steadily developed and ultimately expanded to cordial relations with the Soviet Union, the PRG negotiated five military assistance agreements: three with the Soviet Union, one with Cuba, and one with North Korea. There is some evidence that a military relationship may have also existed with Czechoslovakia and with Bulgaria.

It was naïve of the PRG not to assume that the completion of military agreements with the Soviet Union, Cuba, and North Korea would, almost inevitably, draw Grenada closer to the Soviet bloc, or not to realize that the bloc would expect a quid pro quo. Yet with equal naïveté the Bishop regime stubbornly defended its right to conduct relations and conclude agreements with whatever state it wished. In part, Bishop's actions were motivated by an ever-present fear of invasion from the United States and the need to defend against this.

The extent to which the U.S. government was aware, before the invasion, of the existence of Grenada's military agreements is unknown. Regardless, the Reagan administration discounted the possibility of diplomatic negotiation and chose instead to use economic destabilization, subversion, and the threat of force to return Grenada to Western domination. Thus, Ocean Venture '81 was staged at Vieques near Puerto Rico and utilized 120,000 troops, 250 warships, and more than one thousand aircraft.

The PRG must have felt increasingly threatened by the continued destabilizing pressures from the U.S. and by its own inability to initiate a thaw in relations with Washington, and this was one of the reasons for Bishop's trip to the United States in June 1983. Ironically, Bishop's attempt to mend relations with the United States only served to increase factionalism within the NJM. In the party's Central Committee Bishop increasingly was perceived as soft, indeed, petit bourgeois rather than Marxist-Leninist. The result was a split in the party and, ultimately, the end of the revolution.

Crisis, Disintegration, and Invasion

The struggle between Maurice Bishop and Bernard Coard for leadership of the party and the nation lends itself to analysis on two levels. The first concerns the issue of ideology, or more specifically, the ideological "purity" of the NJM, and the relation of this ideology to the vanguardism promoted by Coard. The second concerns political theory and rhetoric as strategies employed by a particular group within the party (in this case, Bernard Coard's group) to seize power for its own opportunistic ends.

From the beginning the leaders of the coup, in accordance with Leninist theory, appointed themselves the vanguard of the revolution. Although they were willing to forge a temporary alliance with the petit bourgeois business elite to form the PRG, ultimate decisionmaking continued to reside with party members in the Central Committee and in the executive arm, the Political Bureau. During the period of the revolution it was increasingly difficult to gain membership in the NJM. Eventually, the party's links with the masses became more tenuous. To that extent, therefore, it is not entirely surprising that in the final few months of Bishop's regime the leadership corps sought to purge itself further. Indeed, by that time Bishop and a few of his supporters were characterized as petit bourgeois! Vanguardism had come full circle.

The Bishop regime also had to contend with the problem of combining an ideology of social transformation with military force. Having placed itself at the vanguard of the revolution and then having stifled accepted avenues of dissent, the leadership increasingly found it necessary to rely on measures of intimidation. During the last two months of the revolution, especially as arrogance and dogmatism characterized meetings of the Central Committee, a new variant of the socialist model—military socialism—began to emerge in Grenada. The model came into full flower with the establishment of the Revolutionary Military Council in October 1983, with General Hudson Austin as its leader.

The Revolutionary Council was established following the murder of Maurice Bishop and several cabinet members on October 19, 1983, after a struggle for power within the ruling NJM. A number of those on the Central Committee came to disapprove of Bishop's leadership—he was accused of "party indiscipline." The acknowledged leader of those concerned about Bishop's leadership was Bernard Coard. Whereas Coard and his faction had defined the leadership struggle in the context of ideological "purity" and vanguardism, close observers to the dispute agree that the struggle in the party was much more pragmatic—a desire by a particular group to seize power for its own opportunistic purposes. In that context, then, Coard's resignation from the Central Committee simply allowed him time and autonomy to maneuver for leadership. Even so, his wife and other trusted associates remained on the committee.

Coard's attitude toward the working class not only reveals his political motives but also his contempt for that group. He felt the working class should not be involved in decisionmaking and should be kept informed as little as possible. This is hardly a reflection of ideological purity. Both he and his faction consistently argued that the ordinary people should not be involved or informed of the "joint leadership" proposal.[1] As one leader declared, "Joint leadership is an internal party matter and is not to be brought to the masses" (NJM 1983).

The final confrontation between Bishop and the Coard faction regarding the leadership issue occurred at a Central Committee meeting on Sunday, September 25, 1983. This was the last time that the two factions would debate the ideological direction of the party and Bishop's future role in the party. Coard had lobbied the committee members well, for at this meeting in particular, members outdid themselves with Marxist rhetorical excesses. All the "proper" words and phrases were employed. Indeed, linguistic skill appeared almost to be an end in itself. After being thoroughly criticized for his attitudes and his reluctance to endorse the principle of joint leadership, Bishop ultimately appeared to accept, although hesitatingly, that proposal (NJM 1983). Under the proposal Bishop would remain prime minister and be responsible for popular mobilization. Coard, on the other hand, would run the party.

With Bishop and his supporters on the Central Committee visiting foreign countries from September 26 until October 8, Coard consolidated his grip over Grenada both politically and militarily. In order to win the loyalty of the army he granted small salary increases and other benefits. Coard visited all the army camps and did all he could to increase his visibility.

After Bishop's return and his denunciation of the joint leadership proposal it appears that Coard moved increasingly toward a military solution to the question of whether he or Bishop would lead the country. The only meeting held before the Central Committee's decision to place Bishop under house arrest was that of the party branch within the army. At this meeting there was a call for action against Bishop. Bishop and a few colleagues were placed under house arrest on October 13, and for the next six days there followed an intense series of negotiations between George Louison and Unison Whiteman representing Bishop, and Bernard Coard and Selwyn Strachan for the others.

Negotiations for Bishop's release proved ineffective, and thousands of Grenadians, led by high school students, marched to Bishop's home on October 19 and released him from house arrest. Within one hour of his release, the crowd, led by Bishop, congregated at Fort Rupert. Three armored cars appeared on the scene and fired volleys of bullets. The dead, including those who died trying to escape, has been estimated at between fifty and four hundred adults and children. Bishop, three cabinet ministers, and two labor leaders were separated from the group and summarily executed at the fort.

The U.S. Invasion

The militarization of Grenada, which had steadily developed during the four and one-half years of Maurice Bishop's rule, came full circle when some of the same armaments, in the hands of individuals trained under his leadership, were ultimately turned upon him. The revolutionaries killed the revolution, and almost inevitably, the week that followed saw a new level of brutality and repression never before experienced in the country, whose ostensible leadership now consisted of General Hudson Austin and the Revolutionary Military Council. With the invasion of Grenada on October 25 by the United States using enormous military power and about fifteen thousand troops (equivalent to more than 10 percent of Grenada's population), the militarization of the country was now complete.

The fighting itself was brief. U.S. firepower was overwhelming. The force commanded by Rear Admiral Joseph Metcalf III had fifteen vessels, including the USS *Guam* with 609 men and twenty helicopters, the USS *Saipan* with more than twenty-five hundred troops, and the USS *Independence* with seventy-aircraft capacity.

To add an aura of legitimacy to the U.S. forces, because technically the exercise was a joint mission, 300 soldiers and police from six Caribbean countries participated.[2] This politically significant group did not engage in combat but served as guards to the Grenadian and Cuban prisoners.

After two days of brief but sporadically fierce fighting the United States achieved most of its military objectives. The official U.S. figures of those killed in action were United States, 18; Cuba, 24; Grenada, 16. The Grenadian figure did not include the more than twenty people killed when U.S. aircraft accidentally bombed a mental hospital. Officially, more than four hundred on all sides were wounded.

The Aftermath: The U.S., Grenada, and the Caribbean

The granting by the British of independence to Commonwealth Caribbean states since the mid-1960s permitted a power vacuum to develop within the region. As Britain gradually released its hold on these territories, the United States, at least overtly, did not appear in a hurry to take Britain's place. But after Grenada the situation changed dramatically. For if the hegemonic mantle of the U.S. tentatively covered only the Eastern Caribbean before Grenada, today U.S. domination over the region is complete.

The U.S. invasion of Grenada is reminiscent of similar action against the Dominican Republic eighteen years earlier. The consequences also are similar. Hemispheric states have long questioned U.S. respect for the concept of national sovereignty and the principle of nonintervention in state affairs. After the Dominican Republic, the United States, a signatory to the Inter-American Treaty of Reciprocal Assistance (Rio Treaty), lost much credibility, especially within the hemisphere, for its violation of treaty obligations for self-determination. Indeed, during the intervening years, the United States has been closely watched with suspicion. Then came Grenada. Clearly, whatever degree of respect the United States had earned has now been seriously eroded.

A survey of the broad thrust of U.S. foreign policy since 1980 demonstrates that the pursuit of the current conception of national interest, supported by the power of the state, takes clear precedence over international, legal, or moral concerns. To that extent, it may be argued that U.S. action in Grenada does not represent a fundamental departure from traditional U.S. policy toward the hemisphere.

U.S. objectives for the hemisphere traditionally have been twofold: first, that events in the region do not threaten U.S. national security interests; and second, that the region maintain a safe and stable climate for U.S. investments and for the extraction and the passage of raw materials.

Bishop's Grenada threatened both objectives. Domestically, Bishop's national democratic, noncapitalist path sought to promote economic development based essentially upon self-reliance, not upon U.S. investments. To the degree that such a model was successful, it reduced opportunities for U.S. investment; a successful model could have proved attractive to the peoples of the region, all of whom are experiencing deteriorating economic conditions.

Internationally, the national democratic path encouraged Grenada to develop alignments with a long list of anti-imperialist states. Further, Grenada participated fully in the rhetorical war between the East and the West. But Grenada's close alignment with Cuba most caused the United States to be concerned about its peace and security. In the rigid mindset of the Reagan administration, a friend of Cuba was de facto an enemy of the United States, and it is in this context that Cuban support for the building of the new Point Salines airport gained exaggerated significance.

To support U.S. interests and U.S. foreign policy in the region in the aftermath of the Grenada Revolution, increased militarization, and promotion of economic programs that encourage the flow of capital into the region are required. The implications of the latter have already been discussed. What is most obvious, since October 1983, is the haste with which the Reagan administration has moved to establish military-security programs in the region. Even though most of the U.S. troops were withdrawn from Grenada within a few months, U.S. Army and Coast Guard training teams remained. About three hundred Grenadian recruits were trained as a paramilitary Special Services Unit to take the place of the disbanded army. Similarly, a small Grenadian coast guard unit was established with training and equipment provided by the United States.

The United States provided a $15 million military aid package to organize and train Special Services Units in each of the smaller states of the English-speaking Eastern Caribbean. Moreover, the Regional Security System (RSS), a joint security pact between Barbados and the Organization of Eastern Caribbean States (OECS), was revitalized. This culminated in a series of military exercises, the first ever staged in the English Caribbean, in St. Lucia in September 1985. The rationale for this joint U.S.–British–RSS exercise was given by the Barbadian coordinator of the RSS: "We realize that in some situations, we may not be able to deal with the problem by ourselves, and we may have to call for outside help. Therefore we are practicing with the American and British forces to use their equipment depending on the circumstances" (*Caribbean Contact* 1985:2).

The commander of the U.S. Forces in the Caribbean, Admiral Richard Steele, was somewhat more forthright. He stated that the objectives of the exercises were threefold: to practice and refine the training and experience gained during the Grenada operations; to demonstrate the capability of the RSS headquarters; and to demonstrate "the willingness and capability of the democratic nations" to respond quickly to requests for help from a neighbor (*Caribbean Contact*, 1985:2).

Thus, the U.S. penchant for military solutions persists despite the historical problems long associated with that approach: The case of the Dominican Republic is a glaring illustration of the failure of military solutions. James Mitchell, prime minister of St. Vincent, remains a critic of the militarization of the Caribbean, emphasizing that his government "will not spend hard-earned cash to help build a regional army when Vincentians need food, health and proper education" (*Caribbean Contact* 1984:1). Mitchell, nevertheless, remains a lonely voice in a region steadily coopted by the United States and probably will be tolerated so long as he remains unsupported in his views. John Compton, prime minister of St. Lucia, expressed a similar position earlier in this year but quickly changed his mind after an offer of U.S. aid, an increasingly familiar trend in Caribbean affairs (*Washington Report on the Hemisphere* 1985:1).

The immediate future of Grenada and of the Caribbean lies directly with the United States, even more so than in the past. To the extent that the 1979–1983 Grenadian experience was rejected as a viable model, a resurgence of the dependent capitalist approach and, concomitantly, militarization of the region were inevitable. Indeed, the latter approach was implemented within months of the invasion. Although militarization would permit U.S. control in the region in the short term, experience has demonstrated, as in the case of the Dominican Republic, that long-term control is far from assured because the dependent capitalist economic program cannot provide long-range solutions. The Grenada Revolution will remain a possible alternative for Caribbean peoples.

Notes

1. Several months before the 1983 coup, Coard said he could "no longer work with the group under Bishop's leadership because it was not up to the task of building a true Marxist-Leninist party" (Sunshine and Wheaton 1983). The majority of the Central Committee agreed with Coard that Bishop was becoming too powerful as an individual instead of acting as a represesntative of the party. The Central Committee insisted that Bishop submit to "joint leadership" and share power more formally with the Coard faction. The Grenadian people were not informed of the division within the party until it was too late. The party chose to handle the leadership question as an internal manner.

2. The joint mission was supposedly at the request of the Organization of Eastern Caribbean States.

5
Interest Groups and the Military Regime in Suriname

Betty Sedoc-Dahlberg

In February 1980 the civilian government of Suriname was overthrown by a military coup. The military's degree of popularity in the period immediately following the takeover is subject to dispute. However, the growing oppressiveness and brutality of the regime unequivocally reflects its failure to generate popular support. Militarization of the society and a rapidly deteriorating economy on the verge of collapse characterize the regime's rule.

Late in 1979 the armed forces commander and his noncommissioned officers (NCOs) quarreled about the role of the military in the development process and the right of the NCOs to form a labor union. When the sergeants got nowhere with their demands they engaged in a work action, only to be arrested, and their leaders put on trial. On the day they were to be sentenced their comrades came to the rescue, and the result was a nearly bloodless coup. After two years of an uneasy calm, the public began to speak out against the steady rise in unrepresentative extremist groups and to call for the restoration of democracy. By March 1982 violence replaced pressure as confrontations between the military and various interest groups escalated. The climax occurred in December 1982 when the military "defended" the government against an alleged coup attempt by detaining and executing fifteen Surinamese opposition leaders—most representatives of interest groups urging the restoration of democracy.

The Surinamese Army was established at the time of independence in 1975, following considerable debate as to its necessity. The army initially comprised 350 troops and commanded a budget of approximately Sf 13 million (U.S. $7.5 million). The somewhat difficult transition process from a Dutch colonial army geared to controlling internal unrest to a national army with a predominantly developmental orientation took place slowly and had certainly not been accomplished by the 1980 coup.[1] Between 1975 and 1979 plans were developed and implemented to augment the Surinamese defense system with a navy and an air force.

These developments resulted from the perceived need to increase the surveillance of Suriname's marine zone. During this period the army expanded to approximately six hundred troops with a budget of Sf 20 million (U.S. $12 million). By the end of 1983 the Surinamese armed forces numbered more than two thousand, and the budget had increased to more than Sf 65 million (U.S. $43 million). Moreover, with the establishment of the People's Militia in 1982, estimated at three thousand troops, the process of militarization of the society deepened. By 1983 the Surinamese military elite commanded a combined force of 5000 troops in this nation of only 350,000 people.[2]

From 1980 until 1982 Suriname experienced a short-lived economic upsurge due mainly to a substantial influx of Dutch development aid. The so-called Urgent Projects Program allocated approximately U.S. $222 million for priority projects. However, by mid-1982 political developments contributed to a rapid economic decline. The establishment of the People's Militia and the forced resignation by the military of Chin A Sen as president led to a cutback in Dutch aid. This process was accelerated by the suspension of Dutch aid on December 10, 1982, and the cut-off of the much more modest aid programs of the United States and Venezuela following the executions. The cancellation of foreign aid coupled with the decrease in the price of bauxite on the world market led to dire economic consequences for the country. The short-term public debt rose dramatically from U.S. $27 million in 1980 to approximately U.S. $306 million by April 1984. Foreign exchange reserves decreased from U.S. $220 million in 1980 to U.S. $33 million in March 1984. Disastrous financial policies and the drying up of the reserves, a direct consequence of the withdrawal of Dutch aid, contributed to social unrest, which intensified upon the announcement in 1983 of austerity measures required by the International Monetary Fund (IMF) as conditions for future loans.[3]

As a result of the murder of opposition leaders, the country has been the focus of international ostracism. Critical reports on human rights in Suriname by the United Nations, International Labor Office, and the Organization of American States as well as nongovernmental organizations (Amnesty International, the Red Cross, and the International Commission of Jurists) have contributed to the country's isolation. Desperate attempts to remedy this situation have not been successful. At the same time the country is more dependent than ever on foreign resources. The

Dutch have said they will not resume their aid until democracy and human rights are restored.

Political developments have been as unstable as the economy. Between 1980 and 1985 five cabinets have been installed and an estimated fifty-two ministers dismissed. In February 1984 the fourth cabinet was given a mandate to formulate democratic structures for the country. The government was to draft a new constitution for presentation to the public in a referendum to be held in 1985. However, the cabinet's composition (five representatives of the military, two of the labor federations, and two of the private sector) was inherently weak, given the conflicting interests and goals of its constituent members. Any attempts to forge a new constitution and a return to the rule of law and order appear doomed, especially in light of the creation by Suriname's military leader of *Stanvaste*, a political movement proclaimed at the end of 1983 to support the revolution. In November 1984, three thousand people witnessed the official inauguration of the Stanvaste Unity Movement, with Lieutenant Colonel Desi Bouterse, Suriname's military leader, as chairman. Most of the initial membership was from the People's Militia units. Also central to *Stanvaste* and the People's Militia is the Revolutionary People's Party (RVP), a splinter of the Marxist-Leninist party. Because the RVP has infiltrated most institutions within the country, it must be considered an influential political grouping within the country.

To fully understand (1) the success of the coup d'état in 1980 by a poorly disciplined army of 600 troops led by noncommissioned officers, (2) the grip of small, unpopular Marxist-Leninist groups on the country since 1981, and (3) the reaction of the Surinamese people to the increasing militarization of their society, it would be necessary to analyze thoroughly the interconnection of internal and external factors. However, the focus of this study is on the internal dynamics of Surinamese society during the process of militarization.

Two criteria are crucial for the analytical framework used in this period: the degree of control of social life by the military and their constituent organizations, and the degree of military involvement in government decisionmaking. A distinction is made here between "influenced by" and "induced into" a military organization: there are those who for reasons of survival, despite their political rejection of the junta, opt for a certain kind of involvement in the army, and there are others who honestly support the junta. The degree of militarization under examination here is demonstrated by several criteria: the percentage of government expenditure allocated for military purposes; the total personnel serving the armed forces; the level, number, and kind of political positions held by the military; and the status (permanent or temporary) of the military in the decisionmaking process.

In this chapter the process of militarization in the 1980s is defined by the changing stances of interest groups (for example, the labor federations and religious organizations) in the process of the country's transformation from a parliamentary democracy to a military dictatorship. The first section provides a general outline of the political framework, position, and role of the Surinamese Army. Because the focus is on internal factors, the impact of the external environment on the process of militarization is discussed only briefly. The second section analyzes the impact of interest groups on government policy and decisionmaking and the increasing control of social life by the military. The third section deals with the reactions of the junta to increasing protest by interest groups and the absence of substantial support for the newly created policy-formulating and decisionmaking bodies on local and state levels.[4]

Political and Social Framework: From Civilian to Military Government

Suriname became a colony of Holland in 1667. Between 1954 and 1975 the country's status was revised within the Kingdom of the Netherlands, and Suriname achieved some measure of autonomy over its internal affairs. The governor, the representative of the Queen, was retained and was responsible mainly for external affairs. In 1975 the country became totally independent, and the last governor, Johan Ferrier, a Surinamese, became the first president. The new constitution was strongly linked to the Dutch conception of democracy, which is structurally dependent on a House of Parliament, composed of duly elected candidates of political parties.

Before 1980 major political parties were organized predominantly along ethnic lines, corresponding with the three largest ethnic groups—Hindustani, Creole and Javanese.[5] In the last election of 1977 the Creoles' Suriname National Party (NPS) won, together with three small coalition allies, while the Hindustanis' Progressive Reform Party (VHP), with its small partners, gathered in all the remaining seats. The period 1973 to 1977 was characterized by racial polarization in Parliament between Creoles and Hindustanis; both party blocs remedied this by adding new parties from the excluded race to their alliances. The leaders of the ruling parties were known for their patronage politics. There were, however, no sharply defined ideological differences among the parties, and the elected governments were never accused of repression or the use of violence. A certain flexibility and belief in the successful manipulation of people and in effective ethnic sanctions led to the institutionalization of ad hoc policies and allowed a delicate equilibrium of parties/coalitions to control parliament and government. Splinter groups in the 1950s, 1960s and 1970s never seriously challenged the leading parties. Even the Marxist-Leninist parties in the 1970s, originating from radical Surinamese student movements in the 1960s in Holland, did not succeed in obtaining a seat or any leverage in Parliament.

With the military takeover in 1980, the political framework changed drastically. Political parties were banned, the Parliament was suspended, the constitution was adjourned, and elections were postponed. The military proclaimed that it would end racial politics, corruption, and political patronage.

The National Military Council (NMR) was created shortly after the coup to fill the critical role of a guiding body for the new government. The NMR was advised by four small radical parties: the PALU (Progressive Workers and Farmers Union), the Suriname Socialist Union, the Revolutionary Peoples' Party (RVP), and the Nationalistic Republic Party(PNR). The NMR ceased to exist in 1982, and the Political Center was created. This body was chaired by Lieutenant Colonel Bouterse and dominated by the military. Its task was to supervise decisions made by the government. Since January 1984 an exclusively military body, the Military Authority (MA), supported by its civilian advisers, has controlled government decisions. The cabinet is dominated by representatives of the military (five out of nine). A National Assembly—the legislative body—was installed in January 1985. Fourteen representatives of the military, eleven of the labor federations, and six of the industrial associations constitute its members. As a consequence one can conclude that the military formally dominates the legislative and the executive branches of government and has controlled the judiciary since August 1984.

Control over social life by the military and its organizations in the 1980s is apparent. Access to news is limited because of censorship. Open criticism of the regime is considered destabilizing, and critics are likely to be punished. At schools promilitary propaganda is cultivated and the implementation of "ideological" values emphasized. Teachers are instructed by the Ministry of Education, and a significant number of texts and tests for students are prepared in that ministry. The youth militia propagandize in and outside the schools. Control of vital public utility enterprises and the (partial or complete) takeover of the patrol function of the police force in the urban and rural areas by the military lead to a more direct and frequent confrontation of the people with the military. As a consequence of the abolition of political parties and the restrictions under which other interest groups have to function, there is less expression of opinions. These developments contrast sharply with the social and political organization of the country before 1980. In the appendix to this chapter, a selected number of events are presented that underscore the process of militarization in the country.

The Army: Dutch History and Suriname's Future

Until 1975 law and order in Suriname were maintained by about four hundred Dutch personnel, with a few Netherland-trained Surinamese. The issue of a national army received attention only during the independence negotiations in 1974 and 1975. Some advisers thought it better to extend the police force, bearing in mind that Suriname was located on the South American continent and therefore could easily catch the "Latin American disease" of constant coups. Others pointed to the danger of an armed conflict in racially plural Suriname, given the political dominance of the Creole group. After much debate it was generally agreed that a national army would be instituted and would serve a defensive and developmental function. Discussions of the border disputes with Guyana and French Guiana were downplayed. More weight was given to the necessity of protecting the country's coast from "penetrating" fishing vessels. In short, nonmilitary tasks were emphasized and seen as necessary in guaranteeing the contribution of the army to the country's development. In the Charter of the Army the developmental nature of this institution was underscored. But in the aftermath of the 1980 coup, the army's role as a defensive and developmental force was transformed into a directly political function.

In the first years of the young nation it soon became clear that the army was a luxury the country could ill afford; political leaders came to realize how much of the country's resources had to be diverted to the army. The army itself became a "pyramid of frustration" because of the differing and conflicting conceptions of the army that existed among commissioned and noncommissioned officers. The differing conceptions were best illustrated by the aim of the noncommissioned officers for a labor union in the army, a direct cause of the conflicts in 1979 and 1980.[6] Profiles of both groups show that commissioned officers are European-oriented, do not have a clear developmental ideology, are critical of the ill-equipped condition of the army, and are emphatically against societal constraints upon the role of the military. Conversely, the noncommissioned officers objected to the military's hierarchical structure and promotion policies. Those NCOs with linkages to Marxist-Leninist groups functioned after the coup as proponents of the RVP's development policies.

The Military Mission of the Dutch in Suriname, appointed in 1975 in an agreement between the Dutch and Surinamese governments for support and assistance to the Surinamese army, had much to do with the conflict between the commissioned and noncommissioned officers. From its inception the Military Mission was rejected by higher echelons of the Surinamese army, but favored by the lower echelon. According to public statements of Surinamese military now in exile, links between the colonel of the Dutch Military Mission in Suriname and the noncommissioned officers may have contributed to the escalation of conflicts in the army and the increased tensions between the noncommissioned officers and the government.[7] Lieutenant Colonel Bouterse has said that the coup would not have been successful without the aid of key personnel in the Dutch Military Mission.

The junta has been able to maintain state power because of the military support it receives from regional allies. The closest regional allies have been Cuba, attracted by the revolutionary rhetoric of the military leaders, and Brazil, which has sought to counter the Cuban influence and keep the Surinamese government within the capitalist bloc. Cuba's assistance has been essential for the process of militarization in two specific ways. Cuba trained the Surinamese military during 1981, 1982, and 1983 and supported the army and the People's Militia from 1981 to 1983.[8] Cuban aid provided technicians (including military personnel) and advisers on internal security, propaganda, forestry, and health care. Cuban support for the junta continues despite the tensions that developed in late 1983 following the assassination of Maurice Bishop in Grenada.

In a countermove, Brazil, alarmed by the "Cuban line" being followed in Suriname, initiated contact with its neighbor in early 1983. As a result Suriname and Brazil worked out a barter arrangement: Suriname would sell rice and alumina to Brazil in exchange for arms shipments sufficient to allow Suriname's army to double in size. The Brazilians demanded that Cuban-line politics be moderated, and it appears their demands have been taken seriously.[9]

Suriname has entered into the East-West conflict. Nevertheless, the outcome of its political jockeying is that Suriname cannot yet be defined as a satellite state of any of its major backers. But the question remains whether or not Suriname will be able to pursue a politically independent course. By 1984 the original backers of the junta (first the Dutch and later the Cubans) had lost control over the social, economic, and political direction of the Surinamese "revolution."

Increasing control by the army over the affairs of the state and the society was accompanied by a rapid reduction in popular support only six months after the coup. Despite this, the military has not only remained in office but has successfully consolidated its hold over the social fabric of Suriname. Its success in doing so would have been impossible without the active support of the Dutch and leftist governments in the region, and Bouterse has emerged as the most influential individual in the country.

Interest Groups

Decreasing popular support for the government, as demonstrated by the changing attitude of interest groups toward the junta, has resulted in increasing violence and oppression in the country. The growing gap between the junta and popular interest groups is expressed in the statements of labor unions and most importantly in the November 1982 "Open Letter of the Association for Restoration of Democracy" (ARD).[10] The defensive attitude of the junta toward those urging a return to democracy ended tragically in the murders of December 1982. The victims were members of the larger labor federations and/or religious organizations that had played an important role in the political history of Suriname.

Religious Organizations

According to the census of 1972, 41 percent of the Surinamese population are Christians, and 45 percent are Hindus and Muslims. The Roman Catholic church has the largest number of members and is followed in congregational size by the Moravian Brethren and the Lutheran church. These Christian communities are organized in the Committee of Christian Churches (CCK). Among non-Christians the Hindus are the largest religious group. Together with the Muslims, they are organized in the Committee of Hindu and Muslim Communities (CHMG), representing nearly half of Suriname's population. Most of the Christians are Creoles, while the Hindus are of Indian descent, and the Muslims originate from Indonesia and India.

Religious organizations have played a covert but important role in the political history of Suriname. Their interests have paralleled those of the ethnically-based political parties. Church political influence has been maintained through connections with political leaders. By their nature and structure as well as their membership, these interest groups have contributed to racial politics. Spokespersons and leaders of these interest groups have also been involved in politics directly as when they have played a mediating role in cases of conflict between government and labor organizations. Nevertheless, in the past four decades, since the emergence of political parties in Suriname, Christian churches and Hindu and Muslim religious institutions have played a marginal role in the process of development and have generally supported the status quo and political incumbents.[11]

When the military first assumed power and promised to ban corruption and racial politics, to respect U.N. agreements on human rights, and to hold elections not later than October 1982, there was no resistance and criticism from religious organizations. But after six months the church became actively involved when citizens began to call for the restoration of civil and political rights and to question the loss of freedom and the increasing violence. The change in attitude was manifested by articles in church weeklies and Sunday sermons. Discord between the junta and the religious organizations became evident by the end of 1982 when Christian, Muslim, and Hindu organizations were openly called "destabilizing" elements because of their membership in the ARD. Since then these organizations have been excluded from government policy circles.

To understand the reaction of the religious organizations, more specifically the churches, directly after the takeover, the relationship between the religious leaders and the president of Suriname has to be described. In his position as the last governor of the Kingdom of the Netherlands and the first president of the Republic of Suriname, Johan Ferrier had high status and prestige in the country among the several religious denominations. Ferrier generally was accepted by all ethnic groups, and his public acceptance of the military takeover had an important effect on the religious leaders and their members, leading them into silent support for the military regime.

Support for the military-controlled government, however, was short-lived. Several factors contributed to the growing negative reaction by various interest groups including religious groups: Accusations of corruption against the former party leaders and other party members, increasing oppression, and signs that the junta was not in favor of the restoration of democracy influenced the attitude of the religious organizations.

The growing opposition therefore cannot be disconnected from the unfulfilled promises made by the junta on February 25, 1980 to hold elections not later than October 1982, nor can the opposition be seen apart from the increasing influence of the Marxist-Leninist groupings that were known for their hostility toward the old parties. The nomination by the junta of an increasing number of members of the RVP to key positions caused mistrust among the people who saw these new officials as too young, inexperienced, and arrogant. The RVP's Cuban connection also helped to worsen its relationship with the people. Finally, because of the role played by the RVP, including its intensive participation in the People's Militia and the approval of the December 1982 executions expressed by one of its leading members, larger segments of the Surinamese population turned against the junta.[12]

A failing economy and official neglect to prepare for general elections also caused religious groups to sever their support of the junta. Unsuccessful welfare policies in housing and land distribution led to even greater popular disenchantment. The continuation of "pork barrel" politics, whereby only a few persons associated with power elites flourished, was a sharp reminder of the politics of the past. The persistence of these problems indicated that the military regime had violated its own goals and principles.

Labor Federations

Since the mid-1960s the Surinamese industrial and governmental labor force has been organized in four labor federations—namely, the Progressive Workers Organization (PWO), the General Labor Union Federation (de MOEDERBOND), the Centrale 47 (named after forty-seven member unions in the year of proclamation), and the Governmental Workers Organization (CLO). Between 1955 and 1967 the leaders of the two biggest parties, the Creole NPS and the Hindustani VHP, represented wage workers and peasants. Prior to 1967 the two existing and oldest labor federations, PWO and de MOEDERBOND, assumed the role of nonparliamentary opposition movements concerned mainly with a select number of job-related issues (social security, increase of income, secondary facilities).

With the creation of the CLO and the C47 by the tiny, nationalist, socialist-oriented Nationalistic Republic Party (PNR) in 1967, labor unions now appeared to be used by their leaders as tools to challenge government. This has been demonstrated several times when union members were mobilized in tandem with an increase in conflicts between the PNR and the ruling parties. As a Creole-based party, however, the PNR could not successfully compete with the NPS.[13] It lacked popular support and consequently did not succeed in obtaining political power through the labor federations.

Since the end of the 1960s the PWO and de MOEDERBOND have taken a more independent position in disputes with the government. Formally they profess that they abstain from partisan politics, unlike the C47 and the CLO whose stated purpose is to influence government policies specifically and national politics in general. In the 1970s the PWO and de MOEDERBOND, having no partisan affiliation, were in stark contrast to the C47 and the CLO, whose leaders were national representatives of the PNR and held seats in Parliament from 1973 until 1977 when that party participated in the ruling coalition. As a consequence of this union-party link, the PNR had disproportionate representation nationally.

The expulsion of the PNR from the ruling coalition—the National Party Combination (NPK)—by the large NPS and its subsequent loss of every seat in the House of Parliament after the 1977 elections are crucial for understanding the support given by the PNR to the sergeants in the conflict with the government; these factors also explain the subsequent involvement of the CLO

and the C47 as PNR-connected labor federations in the militarization of Surinamese society in the 1980s. The prominence of the
PNR, however, cannot be explained solely by the internal dynamics of the party and by labor politics. The growing importance of
the PNR specifically, and the coup in general, lies in the failure
of governmental policies in the late 1970s. Unemployment and
poverty grew, and the electoral system continued to favor urban
Creoles; additionally, rising expectations of the populace following
independence created the right ambience for the overthrow of the
government.

Between 1980 and 1984 a continuous power struggle emerged
between these various labor federations and against the junta:
PNR leaders tried to benefit from the suspension of the constitution (see Appendix) and made unsuccessful attempts to take
over the country with the aid of the military. The RVP, however,
thwarted those attempts by making certain offers to the military
to consolidate power through support of its connection with Cuba
and other leftist regimes. In the face of a barrage of criticism from
the union rank and file, leaders of the PNR curtailed their support
for the junta in order to maintain a degree of legitimacy.

The leaders of the two older labor federations reacted differ-
ently to the process of militarization in the country. The PWO
leader actively participated in developments in the country under
the military with the hope of garnering benefits, privileges, and
influence for the federation. He was criticized by the members of
the federation who did not wish to give full support to the military.
However, fear of violence from the military for their nonsupport
resulted in only a weak opposition by the members of this federation. In August 1980 the leader of de MOEDERBOND (once
led by the founder and leader of the Creole NPS, Jopie Pengel)
strongly criticized the fundamental violation of civil and political
rights by the junta. In 1982 he urged the restoration of democracy
and the return of the military to its barracks. By that time the
federation had drastically changed its policies and philosophy and
chose to play a clear political role in the country's development. In
the 1982 executions the leader of de MOEDERBOND was killed.

Since 1982 wildcat strikes have spread all across the country;
they are indicative of a rift between the leadership and the rank
and file and a growing politicization of the workers. In a number of
cases disagreements with the power elites and the political system
were cited as the main reason for strike actions. At the end of
1983 this was clear when workers in the bauxite industry kept the
country on strike for seven weeks.[14]

As a result of this pressure the junta leader dismissed the cabinet on January 9, 1984, and installed another consisting of representatives of the labor federations, the private sector, and the military. The new government was given the right to draft a new constitution. The dominance of the military has, however, prevented the construction of an alternative model for democracy. On the contrary, three plans have been drafted for the restoration of democracy, one by each of the three different components of the cabinet. The military, for example, backed by the RVP, presented a plan that was characterized as a model for a totalitarian state, while the privater sector's plan clearly indicated its preference for free elections. In the draft plan of the labor federations the concept of a corporate state was central.[15]

The Surinamese workers seem bent on demonstrating their disenchantment with the junta by striking. Strikes were resumed again in August 1984 and by all accounts will continue on and off indefinitely. Workers are also discontented with their union leadership. The PNR leaders of the CLO and the C47 have political control over the members of their unions, and their success at the bargaining table has contributed immensely to their stay in office. Some de MOEDERBOND workers have criticized the leaders of their federation for weakness, and some of the unions have even considered founding a new labor federation. Bauxite workers who felt betrayed by the rhetoric of the junta threatened strikes unless democracy were restored before the end of 1984. But they were intimidated by the junta and took limited action.

Given the reaction of labor federations to contemporary Surinamese politics, it can be deduced that the country's labor force, including government employees, has changed its attitude from one of support for the government and status quo to an active, openly political role that strives for restoration of democracy and the rejection of totalitarianism. Despite this level of political mobilization, class consciousness has been weak. The middle-class union leadership, once in office, never followed through on its promises to work for democracy. Furthermore, workers' interests remain job-confined, and ethnic conflicts are still alive in the society.

Support for the regime by interest groups such as labor federations and religious organizations is considered a critical pillar of the junta's "new democracy." The junta's dependence on broad alliances without unified ideology has resulted in a failure either to reshape the goals of interest groups or to replace old institutions with newly created bodies. The leaders of the junta have operationalized an "ideology of stabilization" to appease the Surinamese and to obtain the support of leftist regimes within and without the region.

In summary, the executions of December 1982 signified the violent and oppressive atmosphere in the country. The importance of the executions for the analysis of the process of militarization lies in the resulting open, organized mass protest of the union's rank and file supported by large segments of the population who reject political violence.

One effect of the military regime's oppressive tactics might be the emergence of cross-ethnic coalitions on issues of national importance, as expressed, for example, in the "Open Letter of the ARD." But in this ethnically plural society, where people have been split historically into racially defined groups, it is not easy to accomplish a general consensus on values and goals. Still, the circumstances of 1982 are of historical importance for the social history of the country.

The junta has attempted to erode the small gains of unified resistance. For example, organized mass protest resulted in increased importation of weapons and the extension of the People's Militia as well as the development of the youth militia in 1983. The lack of voluntary cooperation from the people has undermined the authority of the junta. As a consequence a state of emergency was implemented and the country ruled by decree. It has become evident that efforts to fulfill the promises made by the junta to the people on February 25, 1980, interfered with the junta's other interests and set precedents that could be used against the people in the future.[16]

The People's Committees

Limited access to existing popular organizations forced the junta to create its own interest groups. Thus, People's Committees (PCs) were created in urban and rural areas by the National Military Council in 1980. The main objective of the PCs was to monitor government policy and to mobilize people in support of the "revolution."[17] Decisionmaking in local politics was to be the responsibility of the PCs (the NMR theorized that democracy should be built slowly at the grass-roots level). PCs were provided with the materials needed to develop their own communities.

Before 1980 similar bodies existed that were linked with the old political parties. They functioned as nuclei for party propaganda and were of crucial importance for political brokers in the patronage politics of the past. With the abolition of political parties after the takeover in 1980 and the junta's accusation of past government corruption, little protest against the proclamation of the PCs appeared. Indeed, the PCs were regarded as alternative new bodies created to replace the old ones but with a similar functon (patronage).

By the end of 1982 the military reported that more than one hundred PCs had been founded.[18] Empirical data on the rise and fall of these organizations are scarce. The military reports that too many PCs have become dominated by members who were not really committed to the new regime. As early as 1981 one army spokesman called the PCs a failure.[19] This condemnation was indicative of the junta's uneasiness with the outcome of the first secret elections in one of the PCs to nominate a board. All members elected were members of the old political parties. The junta thereafter favored nomination of its candidates on the board by open voting, thereby ensuring the nomination of selected loyalists.

Control and supervision of the PCs by the military have always been direct. At the end of 1981 the PCs became members of the newly founded Revolutionary Front. This body was supposed to function as the highest political decisionmaking organ. A lack of support from other interest groups, including labor federations, organizations of peasants and farmers, and women's organizations, contributed to the erosion of the role of the PCs.

It is estimated that only half of the PCs still existed by the end of 1984, and most of these functioned poorly. Decreasing participation in the PCs in mass meetings might be used as an indicator of lack of support by the populace. The power elites appear to distrust the PCs and expect these organizations to play only a marginal role in the consolidation of their regime.

The failure of the PCs is partly a result of poor management. For example, a number of inexperienced persons were nominated to the PCs. Furthermore, poor connections with the centers of decisonmaking in Paramaribo led to uncertainty and delays in decisionmaking within the PCs. The status and position of the leaders of the PCs are, according to some members, too strongly connected to that of the other power elites. This has given rise to tensions between members and leaders and consequently has affected the influence and functioning of the PCs. Rejection and/or sharp criticism of the regime by the labor federations and religious organizations have contributed to reduced support for the PCs. The failure of the PCs has therefore stimulated protesting interest groups to militate for a return to civilian government and general electons.

Conclusion

In the 1980s the Surinamese masses have become increasingly politicized, although this politicization has not been accompanied by a high level of political mobilization. As has been shown in this chapter, the violation of civil and political rights and a deteriorating economy have led to changes in the power and prestige of the leaders of interest groups who hitherto had supported the "revolution." In some labor federations leaders lost control and were confronted with wildcat strikes. In a few cases the workers were able to remove union leaders who were supporters of the new regime. Still, fear of the army and of the People's Militia as well as the military police prohibit sustained public protest. It is within the context of this fear and outrage that the activities of interest groups attain such significance.

Religious organizations in Suriname are usually restricted in their capacity to organize and mobilize citizens for public demonstrations against specific government policies. Church and other religious leaders can influence their members by positions adopted in sermons and in publications but these leaders do not have the instruments to challenge the government in the area of production. Thus, the effects of their opposition are often indirect and take more time to materialize. Labor federations, on the other hand, have used more direct means and are familiar with effective strategies to express their disagreement with government. These interest groups have the capacity to mobilize members quickly and successfully. They indeed forced governments of the pre-1980 period to change their policies.

Several events in the political history of the country have illustrated a support by the other interest groups for labor union activities. Labor union members expect and receive action and leadership from the churches in their protests against the regime. Nonetheless, the power of these groups may weaken as a result of internal competition and conflicting interests. It is significant, however, that in ethnically plural Suriname labor federations have not succumbed to ethnic divisions.

The policies carried out in the 1980s by the military and its advisers resulted in the alienation of large segments of the population and served to galvanize members and leaders of the old competing parties (Creole NPS and Hindustani VHP). Far from reacting positively to these new policies, the populace as represented in the various interest groups is resisting and calling for a return to the partisan politics of the past. The draft plan for restoration of democracy presented to the junta in 1984 was signed by the leaders of the VHP and NPS. Although it was not well received by the junta, the effect on the population after the announcement of the draft plan through a foreign (Dutch) radio station was enough to create feverishly high expectations. The Marxist-Leninist parties will most probably not be able in the near future to radicalize the masses in their favor. The junta members complain about "the weak class consciousness of the people and their low political consciousness," but it also seems that these power elites themselves violate their own policies and therefore contribute to the negative response of the people to their rule.

Appendix to Chapter 5

Some Crucial Events in Suriname (1980-1985)

1980

February	Military takeover
	The NMR (National Military Council) installed
March	The first prime minister of the military government appointed by the president, approved by the military (NMR)
May	Government declaration on Labor Day promising:
	• general elections within two years
	• a law on political parties
	• a new constitution
	• commitment to the preservation of human rights
August	Coup attempt by members of the RVP^a, participants arrested
	President deposed (constitutional)
	Suspension of the constitution
	Abolition of the House of Parliament
	Judicial takeover

1981

January	Issuance of decree regulating power of Policy Center
March	Release of members of the RVP jailed for the coup attempt in August 1980
	"Ideological" takeover
December	Proclamation of the Revolutionary Front

1982

February	Deposition of the prime minister
March	A two-day takeover by Surendre Rambocus and Wilfred Hawker, who promise general elections and military return to barracks
April	Installation of the second military government
June	The creation of a People's Militia consisting of members of the RVP and PALU[a]
	First trained soldiers from Cuba return to Suriname

October/November

Increasing protest of interest groups against oppression and violence

University staff, administrative and technical personnel, and students protest against the junta

Open conflict with de MOEDERBOND

Interest groups urging for Restoration of Democracy and return of the military to barracks

December	Massacre: 15 spokespersons of the people tortured and killed by the junta with involvement of members of the People's Militia
	University of Suriname closed down by the junta
	Abolition of the free press
	Prohibition of newspapers and weeklies and broadcasting corporations
	Cabinet resigns

1983

January	Creation of Anti-intervention Committees (AICs)[b] in industries and business to identify, locate, and fight mercenaries
	Founding of committees to demonstrate solidarity with the "revolution" in parastatal institutions and ministries (with AIC's function)

March	Founding of the youth militia
April	Installation of the third military government, chaired by a member of the PALU; RVP maintains low profile
May	Announcements at Labor Day of the extension of the council network on several levels of policymaking and decisionmaking

September/October

Continuation of replacements of the first and second echelon key positions by members of RVP

Decreasing PALU influence

Announcement of ideological training on local and regional levels by the RVP

November	Proclamation of *Stanvaste*, a political movement; support of all interest groups required, including old political parties[c]
	IMF requirements for loans announced; increasing tension
December	Strikes by workers in the bauxite industry on issues of taxation and democracy; solidarity strikes in the capital accompanied by student strikes (secondary level)
	Opening of the university now ruled by the RVP

1984

January	Continuation of strikes
	The cabinet deposed
February	Installation of the fourth military government, chaired by a formally appointed representative of the Military Authority[d]
May	On request of the Military Authority a "plan for restoration of democracy" presented by the leader of the Hindustani VHP, signed by him and by the leader of the Creole NPS (effect delayed; plan announced three months later by foreign news media)
July	Presentation of three distinct plans for democratic structure to the Military Authority; plans drafted by sections of the military-installed think tank, representing the military, the labor federations, and the private sector; plans reflect conflicting political interests

October/November
  Sequence of strikes on economic as well as political issues

December   Turbulence among workers in the bauxite industries; no strikes

1985

January   Churches openly accuse the junta of violence; people disappear

February   Installation of the National Assembly: Members represent labor federations, the private sector, and the military; private sector represents only local industries and business; others dissatisfied with number of seats

March   Conflict with leader of the C47; junta dismisses C47 representatives from the National Assembly and cabinet

May   Labor union nominees in cabinet no longer considered representatives of these interest groups, but keep seats
  Open hostility of junta toward churches
  Further import restrictions on medicines and foodstuffs
  Transfer of money for students abroad is difficult
  Increasing cases of torture and disappearance

[a] RVP and PALU are two competing Marxist-Leninist parties.

[b] The main objective of these organizations is to identify and report to the military "destabilizing" and "anti-revolutionary" persons who are linked with imperialists and mercenaries.

[c] However, formal political parties have been banned since 1980.

[d] The government is composed of nine members of which five represent the military, two the labor federations, and two the private sector, supervised by the Military Authority assisted by the RVP.

Notes

The author wishes to thank Louk Box for his helpful criticism of an earlier version of this chapter and Carolyn Cooper for editorial assistance.

1. See Slagveer (1980: 20-32). In this report recommendations for changes in the army are put forward by a committee appointed by Prime Minister Henck Arron in May 1979, to investigate conflicts in the army. No attention was paid however to the supporter of the junta. In 1982, nevertheless, he was killed, accused of destabilizing activities in the country.

2. According to Surinamese military who have been in exile since the end of 1983.

3. Following the December 1982 massacre the United States and Holland cancelled aid packages of $1.5 million and $1.5 billion, respectively. In order to acquire a $100 million IMF loan, a 10 percent reduction in state expenditure and a 30 percent devaluation of the Surinamese guilder (official U.S. $1 = Sf 1.80) are required. In 1982 the minister of finance of Suriname, H. Kleine, announced publicly that the junta would not accept these conditions. By 1983, however, the government had instituted IMF-imposed austerity measures.

4. This study is essentially exploratory. Interviews and statistical documents as well as other primary and secondary data are used. The methodological approach, however, is based on analyses of networks relevant for political decisionmaking; and focuses on the change of position of interest groups and the nature of the relationship of the leaders with members of these groups. Historical similarities between Suriname and other Caribbean countries are significant. However, this study is not expansively comparative. Occasional references are made to other Caribbean countries.

5. For a discussion of the ethnic groups in Suriname and the role played by ethnicity in politics, see Dew (1976); and Sedoc-Dahlberg (1983).

6. For a more detailed description of the 1980 coup, see Verhey and van Westerloo (1983).

7. Colonel Valk, head of the Dutch Military Mission, confirmed his involvement in the February 1980 coup in an interview with Verhey and van Westerloo (1982).

8. For more information about Cuba's increased interest in Suriname, see *The Nation* (1984).

9. See *Miami Herald* (1983); and *Latin America Weekly Reports* (1983).

10. See *De Ware Tijd* (1982).

11. Historically the churches adopted an attitude of government support or, in cases of disagreements, nonpublic protest. For example, with regard to strategies used to carry out innovations in primary and secondary education during the 1970s, there was disagreement but no protest.

12. The massacre was described as a needed "shock-therapy," according to Sewrajsing (forthcoming).

13. See "C47:Vijf en Twintig Jaren Strijd" (1984).

14. See *NRC-Handelsblad* (1984).

15. See Consortium of Labor Federations (1984).

16. See Slagveer (1980); and Verhey and van Westerloo (1983).

17. According to an interview with J. Sital (1981).

18. As reported in Sital (1981).

19. Sital (1981).

6

The Role of the Military in the National Security of Guyana

George K. Danns

Militarization of a society in a Third World context is a visible and common response by its rulers to perceptions of threats to national security, both external and internal. In a broad sense, national security refers to any effort, policy, or program introduced and/or implemented by a government in power (1) to protect the country's borders against external aggression and the nation's resources and people against plunder; (2) to insulate the government itself against armed overthrow or subversion; or (3) to resist any action viewed as contrary to the government's definition of national interest. National security as a concept applies to perception, interest, and action. The powerful nations see a threat to their national security everywhere in the world where the ideology, policies, and way of life of other countries are at variance with theirs.[1] Analytically, national security can be considered from two separate though related standpoints: problems of internal security and order and problems of and threats to external security.

As an action response to the perceived needs of national security, militarization is a condition in which increasingly large portions of the population and the society's resources become progressively involved and dominated by, or inducted in one way or another into, military and paramilitary institutions. Militarization is a political condition in which military-type institutions are viewed by a ruling elite as an organizational panacea for the "ills" of external defense, indiscipline, social instability, and problems of mobilization, control, and development within a society. Militarization also is a social condition in which regimentation is seen as a way of life.

Guyanese society represents a significant illustration of growing militarization as a direct response to national security needs. Externally, the country faces several claims on its territory by its adjacent neighbors, particularly from Venezuela on its northwestern border. Internally, the authoritarian People's National Congress (PNC) regime has established one-party dominance and adumbrates policies that are unpopular and resisted even by some of its own supporters. A state-controlled economy that is caught in a deep economic recession adds to problems of internal security. The regime relies on its broad-based military apparatus to sustain its rule and enforce its unpopular measures. With such excessive demands of both internal and external security on this small nation, Guyana has emerged as probably the most militarized of Commonwealth Caribbean countries in terms of the ratio of military personnel to citizens, the proportion of national resources expended on the military, and the number and variety of military institutions.

Military developments in independent Guyana are direct outcomes of the policies of the incumbent People's National Congress regime. When the PNC party assumed office in coalition with the right-wing United Force (UF) party after the December 1964 elections, there existed two military institutions—the British Guiana Police Force and the Special Service Unit (SSU). Currently, there are five different military and paramilitary institutions in Guyana.

Table 6.1

Estimated Organizational Strength of Security Forces

Military Unit	Estimated Organizational Strength			
	1964	1966	1977	1984
Guyana Defense Force *	500	750	4,000	4,500
Guyana Police Force	1,635	1,881	3,751	4,208
Guyana National Service	–	–	4,000	4,500
Guyana People's Militia	–	–	1,000	2,500
National Guard Service	–	–	–	2,000
Total	2,135	2,631	12,751	17,708

* In 1964 the Guyana Defense Force was known as the Special Service Unit (SSU).

Source: Figures on the police force were obtained from Government of Guyana (1976; 1984), and personal interviews.

Table 6.1 provides the estimated strength of the armed forces in Guyana. The strength of the British Guiana Military in 1964 was 2,135, representing a ratio of 1 military personnel for every 300 citizens. Between 1964, when the PNC regime came into office, and 1984, the military has grown by 829 percent to 17,708. This represents an average yearly increase of 779 personnel. With an

114

estimated population of 759,000, the ratio of military personnel to civilians stands at 1 military personnel for every 43 citizens.

Expenditure on the military parallels the increase in variety and size of military institutions during the years. Tables 6.2a and 6.2b provide figures on expenditures on the military between 1973 and 1984. In 1973 the government expended a total of G $22,494,569 (U.S. $4,998,793) on the military, and for 1984 the budget was G $166,429,000 (U.S. $36,984,222), representing an increase in defense spending of more than 600 percent. In 1973 defense spending represented 7.7 percent of the national budget, and by 1976 this had increased to 14.2 percent. Currently, expenditures on the defense forces are estimated at 11 percent of the national budget. It is quite possible that much more is expended on the various military institutions than is reflected in the annual budget releases of the government. The army allegedly exports gold to purchase arms. In fact, the national budget allocations for the military exclude expenditures for arms and ammunition, which are purchased externally.

During the years the Guyana government has, however, been expending more on the military than in any other single area of state activity. In 1984 the government budgeted a total capital and current expenditure of G $58,375,000 (U.S. $12,972,222), or 3.5 percent of the national budget, for health care services. Similarly, the government budgeted a total of G $104,440,000 (U.S. $23,208,888), or 6.3 percent of the national budget, for education. That is, the government spends and allocates more money on the military than on the health and education of the nation combined.

Agriculture has been proclaimed by the regime as the key to transforming the nation's unfortunate economic circumstances and bringing about economic development. A "grow more food" campaign has been launched, and people are being encouraged to plant in their yards and on the parapets. More and more lands are being released by the government for farming, and external loans and aid have been sought and in some cases obtained for agricultural development. In view of the agricultural drive, it would be normal to expect that agriculture would be a major area for state investment and expenditure. This, however, is not so. In 1984 the government budgeted for agriculture a total capital and current expenditure (inclusive of Inter-American Development Bank aid) of G $127,226,000 (U.S. 28,273,333), representing just 7.7 percent of the national budget. In spite of the agricultural base of the

Table **6.2**<i>a</i>

Expenditure on Military Institutions, 1973–1975 (G$)
(in millions)

Military Institutions	1973	1974	1975
Guyana Defense Force	10.12	17.86	32.71
Guyana Police Force	12.37	13.31	15.70
Guyana National Service	–	6.49	30.50
Guyana People's Militia	–	–	–
National Guard Service	–	–	–
Total	22.49	37.66	78.92
Percent of National Budget	7.7%	10.6%	13.5%

Source: Government of Guyana (1976).

Table **6.2**<i>b</i>

Expenditure on Military Institutions, 1976–1984 (G$)
(in millions)

Military Institutions	1976	1982	1983	1984
Guyana Defense Force	64.09	74.13	78.70	77.99
Guyana Police Force	18.74	36.72	41.78	42.44
Guyana National Service	20.50	24.37	30.00	33.00
Guyana People's Militia	9.80	*	*	*
National Guard Service	–	6.48	5.00	13.00
Total	113.14	141.70	115.48	166.43
Percent of National Budget	14.2%	8.7%	11.61%	10.6%

* Budgetary allocations for the Guyana People's Militia (GPM) are subsumed under that of the GDF.

Source: Government of Guyana (1977; 1984).

country's economy and its great potential for agricultural development, the government, relative to investments in the military and evidenced by its budgetary allocations, has not been supporting agricultural development as espoused in its policy statements.

The preeminent role given to the military in the national life in Guyana should not, however, lead one to overestimate the military's capabilities. Guyana is a poor, underdeveloped nation, and its military reflects this poverty and underdevelopment. The Guyana military is ill-equipped, and its warfare and defense technology are relatively backward. The military in Guyana consists almost exclusively of ground forces. There are no air force and navy. The Guyana Defense Force has only a tiny air wing consisting of a few small transport aircraft and a marine wing consisting of a few small vessels. An examination of the five military institutions provides further understanding of their essential function in national life in general and national security in particular.

The British Guiana Police Force was established in 1839 by the British immediately following emancipation of the slaves after the freed blacks had fled the plantations for the villages and towns. Police stations were set up along the coastlands of Guyana where the great majority of the population live and were established almost exclusively in black communities. Along with the planters and the militia, later the British Guiana Volunteer Force, and subsequently in 1964 the Special Service Unit, the police were responsible both for internal security and for the security of the country's borders.[2] These are still the essential functions of the police, and the police still maintain outposts for border protection around the country. Since Guyana became independent and a republic, the police have been renamed the Guyana People's Police, and government leaders have called upon the police to be involved in national development efforts. The police have established farms, a credit union and a consumer cooperative. Their responsibility for law enforcement and order maintenance, however, occupy most of their efforts. Whereas in the colonial era the police were the first and principal line of defense for matters of internal and external security, today there are several other military institutions so involved (Danns 1982).

On November 1, 1965, the government, under the leadership of the late Forbes Burnham, was allowed by the British to transform the SSU into a full-fledged army—the Guyana Defense Force (GDF). The Guyana Defense Force was set up, organized, and trained by British Army officers. Officer cadets were sent to Mons and Sandhurst military academies in Britain. With the setting up of the local army, the British garrison that had been sent to the colony in 1964 to aid the local security forces in quelling racial and industrial riots withdrew.

The role of the army was defined as follows:

1. to maintain the integrity of the borders of Guyana and to defend against aggression;

2. to assist in the maintenance of law and order in Guyana when required to do so;

3. and to contribute to the life of the country by organizing voluntary services, engaging in engineering and other projects, and providing a labor rescue organization in an emergency (Danns 1983:80).

In addition, Forbes Burnham, then prime minister, minister of defense, and chairman of the defense board, called on the army to be personally loyal to him, his party and its policies, and the government. The army was expected to:

1. repudiate the doctrines of capitalism, elitism, self-indulgence, and economic oppression and proclaim cooperative socialism;

2. unite the officers and men of the GDF with the broad masses of people of Guyana so that the GDF became a "people's army" and the masses became the "army's people";

3. and support the government to the end and implement its policies unhesitatingly (*The Scarlet Beret* 1971:14).

From its inception, the army in independent Guyana had a responsibility both for national security and for national development.

In 1973 the Guyana government established the Guyana National Service (GNS). It is a military organization designed to attain the following objectives:

1. provide training and skills that are consistent with national needs;

2. increase national production;

3. provide workers for development;

4. achieve self-reliance;

5. develop and populate the hinterland;

6. develop an understanding of national objectives;

7. coordinate rescue and relief operations during national disasters, emergencies, or catastrophies;

8. unite the various racial, social, and economic groups in Guyana for their survival and development;

9. and assist in national defense.

The Guyana National Service was as much an institution for defense as it was an institution for bringing about development. The GNS was supposed to be a training ground for the "new Guyana man"; its organizational influence extended to the schools, the teachers' colleges, and the local university. Its pioneer corps created opportunities for the employment and training of unemployed youths. The GNS also has a special service corps for enlisting professionals and technically skilled people and a National

Reserve Corps in which graduates of the institution may be called up for purposes of national defense or in the event of any national disaster or major internal security threat.

GNS settlements were deliberately set up in the interior regions of the country as part of a long-term plan to establish settlements of people and organized military communities along or near Guyana's borders. The Guyana National Service was able to focus in a more deliberate and sustained fashion on development programs. This military organization so far has six settlements in various parts of the country's interior that are involved in large-scale farming of legumes, citrus and cotton crops, a dairy industry, and gold and diamond mining as part of a growing spectrum of economic activities. Its attention to military functions is by no means neglected, however. GNS personnel are trained by the army, and indeed some army personnel have been seconded for this purpose. The current chief of staff of the armed forces in Guyana, Brigadier Norman McLean, was the first director general of the GNS. Since then two army officers, Colonel Desmond Roberts and, presently, Colonel Joe Singh, have headed the GNS. It has been said that the Guyana National Service has direct responsibility for the protection of Guyana's eastern borders.

Three years after having established the GNS, the regime established yet another military institution. The Guyana People's Militia (GPM) was set up in 1976 with the expressed aim of making "every citizen a soldier," thus making possible a large reservoir of people skilled in soldiering on behalf of national security. The militia's purpose is:

1. to provide a framework in which mass preparations for emergencies can be carried out during periods of rising tensions;
2. to support the People's Army in all of its functions as needed;
3. to assist the People's Police in the maintenance of law and order as needed;
4. to provide a reservoir of recruits for the army;
5. and to contribute to the life of the community by engaging in productive work and providing a labor rescue organization in an emergency.

The Guyana People's Militia is in the main a part-time reserve military body somewhat like the defunct British Guiana Volunteer Force. It is an auxiliary arm of both the army and the police and also has a responsibililty for bringing about national development. With the police, the army, and the GNS already established, it was not altogether clear why the PNC government set up yet another military institution. The GNS had within its organizational ambit provision for part-time and standby military personnel. The Guyana People's Militia functions more in practice as a reserve for the GDF and is designed as a community military organization aimed at boosting the military and national security capabilities of the nation.

The National Guard Service (NGS) is yet another military institution said to have originated in 1980 in response to a need to guard and protect government offices and state property against theft and acts of economic subversion. The Burnham government began to express alarm about what appeared to be subversive acts aimed at inhibiting the effective functioning of new state economic entities such as the Sanata Textile Mill. Sugar crops already had been prematurely burned by arsonists, and other actions designed to thwart production in state enterprises were thought to be increasing at an alarming rate. Deputy Commissioner of Police Laurie Lewis (who was also a deputy director of the GNS) had some connection with the intelligence branch of the police force and was specially assigned to deal with such problems. The National Guard Service grew out of his organizational efforts. Previously, state organizations either recruited their own watchmen and security or else relied on private security agencies. The watchmen and security personnel attached to state offices and agencies were coopted into the National Guard Service, and additional fresh guardsmen and guardswomen were also recruited and equipped with a distinctive military uniform and other appurtenances. The state, through policies of nationalization, owned an increasingly larger portion of the economy (estimated at more than 50 percent), and protection of state property became imperative. Guardsmen and guardswomen are posted at government offices, schools, ministries, corporations, hospitals, and health centers. The National Guard Service from all appearances is also providing security services for a few foreign missions. National Guard personnel are publicly acknowledged and awarded for acts of bravery and exceptional vigilance.

The National Guard Service currently has an organizational establishment of 2,000 personnel with many possibilities for growth as efforts to regularize security arrangements in state agencies not coming under the jurisdiction of other military bodies succeed. Little is known about what the finances of the organization were during its formative stages. In 1982, however, a sum of G $6,483,298 (U.S. $1,440,733) was appropriated for this agency and in 1983 a sum of G $5,000,000 (U.S. $1,111,111) was given. The money allocated by the government in 1984 was G $13,000,000 (U.S. $2,888,849), thus indicating the seriousness with which this military organization is treated.[3]

Despite the appropriation of government funds, the National Guard Service is not yet a legal entity, although its arms and ammunition are legally registered, nor is the NGS a registered company or a public corporation. It is not a government department, nor is it publicly acknowledged as a branch of the disciplined forces. Further, its parameters and principles for operation are yet to be specified and are at best emergent. Its undefined nature has sparked unsubstantiated rumors of its being an intelligence agency. Although the careful monitoring activities of the NGS can and probably are used for intelligence purposes, there are as yet no firm grounds for defining it as an intelligence agency.[4] The lower ranks of the guard service are persons with hardly more than a primary education, while its officer ranks are attracting young and qualified persons as well as retired police officers.

Threats and Problems of External Security

The establishment and maintenance of five separate military institutions by the Guyana government underlie what has become a policy for the militarization of the society in which, as decreed in the motto of the GPM, "every citizen is a soldier." It is clear that the PNC government, which proclaims a socialist orientation, copied the policies of other socialist countries, most notably Cuba, which also instituted such a variety of military bodies. Without developing a navy and an air force, the Guyana government sought variety in its ground forces. This "marching" strategy of militarization was seen by the regime as necessary to protect "the gains of the revolution" by resisting imperialist forces from without and reactionaries from within from thwarting its socialist, nonaligned, self-reliant, and progressive thrust. The PNC regime and its leadership, convinced of their seemingly preordained revolutionary role in the history of Guyana, are unprepared to compromise Guyana's sovereignty and are even more resistant to yielding power through democratic or other means to any alternative group in the society.

Guyana, however, faces very real external threats to its national security. These threats stem from its neighbors—Venezuela, Suriname, and Brazil—all of which resurrected territorial claims against Guyana shortly before or since it acquired independence. The threat from Venezuela, its much bigger and stronger western neighbor, is by far the most serious and the most imminent.

The government of Venezuela resurrected a territorial claim against Guyana in 1962, just prior to independence.[5] The British government had settled the territorial dispute by an 1899 Arbitral Award, but the Venezuelan government of Raoul Leoni declared the 1899 award null and void and launched a campaign to claim five-eighths of Guyana's territory. On February 17, 1966, the governments of Great Britain, British Guiana, and Venezuela signed a Geneva Agreement establishing the Guyana-Venezuela Mixed Commission whose explicit purpose was to find "satisfactory solutions for the practical settlement of the controversy." The Mixed Boundary Commission, as it became known, had four years to complete its work. The new nation of Guyana was born on May 26, 1966, with a legacy of discord with its relatively mighty Venezuelan neighbor.

In October 1966, in violation of the spirit of the recently signed and enacted Geneva Agreement, the Venezuelan army invaded Guyana. Since then it has occupied Guyana's eastern half of the island of Ankoko in the Cuyani River. The small Guyana Defense Force was no match for the Venezuelan armed forces and made no effort to engage the Venezuelan army in combat. The Guyana government resorted to diplomatic channels and international lobbying to keep Venezuela from encroaching farther. This, however, did not stop the Leoni government from issuing a decree in July 1968 that was intended to allow Venezuela to claim a nine-mile portion of Guyana's territorial waters. The Leoni decree authorized the Venezuelan military to enforce the claim.

The Venezuelan government accompanied its aggressive territorial claim with attempts at economic destabilization. While the Guyana government was negotiating funding for a hydroelectric project in the Upper Mazaruni, the Venezuelan government issued a full-page advertisement in the *London Times* warning prospective investors not to get involved in any business ventures in those areas of Guyana being claimed by Venezuela.

Again, on February 23, 1970, on the occasion of the country's celebration of its new republic status, "the Venezuelan Armed Forces launched a mortar attack on one of Guyana's border posts" (Jackson 1982:17). The Guyana military did not return fire, and diplomatic protests were lodged.

The Guyana-Venezuela Mixed Boundary Commission completed its work in February 1970 without reaching an accord on the territorial dispute. Diplomacy has been described as "war by other means"; Guyana's diplomatic offensive in international forums produced some positive results. Guyana was declared a republic within the Commonwealth on February 23, 1970, and in June 1970 the Protocol of Port-of-Spain was signed between the governments of the Republic of Guyana, Venezuela, and the United Kingdom. Trinidad's illustrious leader, the late Eric Williams, aided this process considerably, and by this new agreement Guyana and Venezuela decided to freeze or suspend for twelve years the issue of the territorial claim and to work toward better relations between the two countries. Venezuelan president Carlos Andres Perez visited Guyana in 1978. Earlier in 1975 a cultural agreement was signed, and with the visit of the Venezuelan president some measure of aid and trade followed.

In early 1979 the regime of Carlos Andres Perez was replaced by that of Luis Herrera Campins. This change of rule signaled the resumption of hostilities toward Guyana. In a disastrous state visit to Caracas on April 2-3, 1981, the late president Burnham was embarrassed by "an orchestrated Venezuelan campaign of hostility towards Guyana, including strident calls for military occupation of the region claimed and the institution of a naval blockade of Guyana" (Memorandum on the Guyana/Venezuela Boundary 1981:14). Less than twenty-four hours after President Burnham had left, President Herrera issued the following statement from Caracas:

1. Both Chiefs of State held cordial and frank talks on relevant issues and on matters of current international interest.

2. President Herrera firmly ratifies Venezuela's claim to the Essequibo territory. An illegal arbitration award of 1899, which was never valid, despoiled Venezuela of that territory.

3. President Herrera thus reiterates Venezuela's rejection of any compromise incompatible with Venezuela's claim and stresses the nation's desire that the grave injustice committed against it by the voracity of the colonial empires should be righted. For the same reason President Herrera reiterates Venezuela's rejection of the hydroelectric project of the Upper Mazaruni.

4. President Herrera also reiterates that Venezuela and Guyana are committed to seeking practical and satisfactory solutions to the pending controversy and rati-

fies Venezuela's determination to continue exploring every means to achieve that end. Therefore, for the record, he states at this moment, Venezuela was not willing to extend the Port-of-Spain Protocol (Memorandum on the Guyana/Venezuela Boundary 1981:14-15).

Forbes Burnham, in an earlier speech to the Guyana Parliament in 1968 after Venezeula had annexed Guyana territorial waters, had said:

I cannot tell with any certainty where this ill-advised course of action on which the Government of Venezuela has embarked will lead us. We must be prepared, however, for further and even more aggressive demonstration of international lawlessness from the Government of Venezuela. We will need all our courage and strength to withstand these efforts to break our will and despoil our land. Venezuela has now made clear its intention to seek relentlessly to re-impose the yoke of colonialism on a small nation that has succeeded in freeing itself from the tutelage of another imperial power. We have no quarrel with the Venezuelan people, but we shall not lack courage or resolve in resisting aggressive demands of a Venezuelan government that is prepared to defile the traditions of Bolivar and to flout the precepts of hemispheric and world order and security (Memorandum of the Guyana/Venezuelan Boundary May 1981:19-20).

Burnham's speech and the government's appeals to international forums and the nations of the world have not, however, stopped Venezuela's aggression against Guyana. Nor have the five military institutions supporting the government displayed any willingness to stand up to the might of the Venezuelan armed forces.

It should be apparent that neither the size of the Guyana security forces nor the funds expended to equip it are adequate when the threats to Guyana's national security by Venezuela's territorial claims and the atmosphere of military aggression pervading the international environment are considered. The problem is, however, that Guyana can ill afford to expend many more of its scarce resources on the military and withdraw them from other development priorities. The ill-equipped military in Guyana cannot match its more powerful neighbors and would be unlikely as presently constituted to repel effectively any determined and sustained attack from one of its more powerful neighbors or any sizable and well-equipped invading forces. Nevertheless, military officials in Guyana state that they are capable of holding at bay for a while any invading force until either "help" arrives or else diplomacy and international condemnation halt the aggressors. Further, they see the military as an effective deterrent to minor incursions into Guyana's territory and an armed reminder to all that "Guyana is not Grenada."

The argument can be made, however, that the organization of the military in Guyana is not geared to obtaining maximum use of resources for the purpose of external defense. The paucity of foreign exchange to obtain military hardware has inhibited the setting up of an air force and a navy. Ground forces are unsuited for purposes of protecting Guyana's airspace and territorial waters. The Guyana government accused the Venezuelan government of violating Guyana's airspace eighty-odd times in 1982. Venezuelans have been bullying Guyanese using the Cuyuni River, which falls within Guyana's territory. Venezuelan and other foreign fishing fleets have been illegally invading Guyana's territorial waters and stealing its marine resources. In 1983 a couple of Venezuelan trawlers were captured in Guyana's territorial waters by the marine wing of the army. More recently a fleet of fifty South Korean and other foreign fishing vessels were seen in Guyana's waters. Three were captured, and one South Korean sailor was killed in the process. The point is that unless efforts are made to develop an air force and a navy, the economic security of the country will be further undermined, and its defense capabilities will remain suspect.

Guyana's other two neighbors, Brazil and Suriname, also staked claims to the country's territory after its independence. Brazilians seem to have given up their claims or at least rested the matter for the time being. Brazil has since developed ostensibly friendly relations with Guyana, and there is sizable trade between the two countries, particularly in the area of thriving underground economic activities. The Brazilian government is also giving aid and technical assistance to Guyana, including military training for the Guyana Defense Force and other forms of military aid. Brazil also is apparently supportive of Guyana's assertion of its territorial rights and strongly objects to a military solution to the Guyana-Venezuelan border dispute.

The Brazilian initiative was not, however, one favored by Guyana's neighbor to the east—Suriname. In 1969 the Guyana Defense Force was pressed into combat to recapture the New River Triangle in Corentyne, Berbice from some Surinamese who had arbitrarily invaded and had plans to establish a large-scale settlement. The army, assisted by the police, for the first time was able to successfully overcome direct efforts by a neighboring country to seize a portion of Guyana's territory. With the constant or probable threat of Guyana's three neighbors—Venezuela, Suriname, and Brazil—all staking claims to the country's territory, border defense has become a principal and preoccupying aspect of the role of the military in external security.

The relative weakness of the Guyana military does not, however, stop the PNC government from providing "military assistance" to some Commonwealth Caribbean countries and even farther afield to African countries fighting liberation struggles. GDF soldiers were allegedly sent to Dominica during a minor insurrection involving Rastafarians and radical socialist intellectuals. Again, GDF officers were allegedly involved in planning and executing military strategy that enabled Maurice Bishop and the New Jewel Movement to successfully overthrow the Gairy regime in Grenada. The Guyana military also assists in cadet officer training for some of its Caribbean neighbors. Despite warnings from the United States, the Guyana government allegedly permitted Cuban aircraft en route to Angola with troops to refuel at the Timehri International Airport. Allegations were also made that Guyanese troops may have been involved in African liberation struggles. It is definitely known that monetary contributions were given to Joshua Nkomo's organization during Zimbabwe's liberation struggle.

The external involvements of the Guyana military and the problems of external defense are very much related to the foreign policies of the government. Essentially, the Guyana government seeks to foster an image as an independent, nonaligned, progressive, and socialist society with no underlying ties to either East or West. The government calls for a redefinition of the international economic order and for cooperation among Third World countries to transform their circumstances. The government is against racism and apartheid, colonialism, the acquisition of territory by force, and the armed intervention in the affairs of other countries. In pursuing its foreign policies, the Guyana government has been seeking to maintain a high profile of involvement in international forums such as the United Nations and its various organs, support freedom fighters in Africa, and join both intra- and extraregional organizations for economic cooperation.

The government's pursuit of a policy of nonalignment, of being in neither the East nor West blocs, may be important for a sense of national integrity for a small, underdeveloped nation-state, but it may also be at variance with the realities of international power politics and can be viewed as either conceit or courage on the part of the regime and its leadership. What is clear is that Guyana's nonalignment puts it in the unenviable position of having no dependable friends and several reliable enemies. The truth is that Guyana cannot be assured of any rescue or aid in the event of an invasion by Venezuela, any of its other neighbors, or the United States. It cannot look forward to military assistance from the Caribbean Community (CARICOM) countries or from elsewhere. In real terms, nonalignment for Guyana means loneliness and friendlessness. The Guyana military in general and its army in particular are unhappy with this aspect of the government's foreign policy but dare not openly voice their concern. As one army officer said, "We are frightened as hell at the prospect of having to withstand, unaided, a large-scale military attack." Denunciations in international forums would be small comfort for the vulnerable military if such a situation should arise. In this sense, the Guyana government's foreign policy is at variance with the realities. There can be no realistic concept of external security outside of a framework of a military alliance with other countries. Just as the domestic policies of the regime have perplexed social and political relations and frustrated economic growth, so, too, the regime's foreign policies may be endangering the very survival of Guyana as an independent nation-state.

Problems of Internal Security

The problems of internal security of a nation-state are essentially problems of order. Order maintenance in new nations such as Guyana is very often a difficult proposition for postcolonial rulers. Problems of competitive alliances for power among ethnic, tribal, religious, and class groupings may keep new nations in prolonged ferment. Arriving at and maintaining legitimate consensus on new or changed systems of postcolonial rule are very often the crux of the conflicts of order in such societies. The dominant trend has been for leaders with narrow partisan or sectarian interests to seize or hold onto power through undemocratic means. Military machinery created in the postcolonial era to support authoritarian and neofascist regimes very often gives rise to vested organizational interests, and the military often seizes power for itself.

The dominant one-party rule of the PNC regime in a multiple party system is very much cast in this trend of undemocratic rule in the Third World. Through the rigging of national and local elections and various constitutional manipulations, the regime has maintained a stranglehold on the postcolonial state apparatus and on the society. The regime has promulgated the doctrine of party paramountcy over the government and has made the captive state system a party state. Extensive policies of nationalization leading to state ownership of more than 50 percent of the economy have strengthened the control of the regime. A socialist ideology has been advanced, and the official title of the country is The Cooperative Socialist Republic of Guyana. State-controlled public enterprises have been managed into virtual bankruptcy, and the economy as a whole has been caught in a vortex of recession and decay.

Guyana has become, since the mid-1960s, a very troubled society. Unemployment stands at an estimated 30 percent of the work force. Wages paid by the state are far below the very high cost of living, and growing industrial unrest has for the moment been headed off by labor legislation that virtually outlaws strikes and other forms of industrial protest. Galloping inflation and shortages of essential commodities due to major reductions of imports by the state have added to the torment of the Guyanese people and fueled the emergence of a viable underground economy. Efforts by other political parties and other concerned groupings to mobilize the masses are continually being negated and neutralized by the regime's use of the military and other extralegal party groups to violently discourage opposition. The regime does not feel obligated to account to the public for its policies and actions. Serious crises of legitimacy, credibility, and accountability confront the postcolonial state. The morale of the nation has been shattered by the regime's arrogant use of power and recalcitrant attitude to public demands for policy changes. People have been withdrawing from the society in increasingly large numbers and in general have rejected the regime's rule, condemned its widespread corruption, and criticized its "socialist thrust."

Because the PNC regime holds onto power at all costs and imposes its will despite popular dissent (such as the growing underground economy and low voter turnout at national elections), it has of necessity to rely on the military to preserve the status quo. In general, the military in Guyana is a serious impediment to any democratic succession to the regime.[6] The military gives the regime an aura of omnipotence and permits the leadership of the government to adumbrate policies that are both unpopular and repressive. The military forms an integral and potent segment of the burgeoning state apparatus, and its members have been assuming a growing sense of their own importance in the society and of their stake in preserving the status quo. Former president Burnham, as commander in chief of the armed forces, fostered this sense of importance among the military by allegedly assuming the highest rank and membership in each military branch, with the exception of the National Guard Service. Further, in what appears to be a rhetoric of deception, he called on the military to be leaders in the community and leaders in the society.

The nature and organizational diversity of the military ground forces in Guyana lead one to question whether the government's focus is more on the internal rather than the external aspect of national security. Guyana's defense forces have been designated a role in the economic development of the country.[7] The argument has been made that an army in the Third World is an expensive venture, and a country cannot afford to sit and wait for war or else engage its army in costly "war games" around the world. Instead, it is argued that the minds and energies of the army's men and women must be directed to developing the nation's resources.

Notwithstanding the defense forces' involvement in development projects, the focus of the defense forces does seem primarily oriented to the preservation of the regime, rather than to any other consideration. Even the GDF is involved in the internal security of the regime. At national elections the army involves itself in transporting ballot boxes in convoys around the country and denies opposition political parties the right to verify the ballot count. Army officers have to pledge their personal loyalty to the "comrade leader" and are expected to, and do, take part in PNC party congresses. The army also conducts military maneuvers in the various communities of the nation just prior to an election or to the passing of some austere bill or budget. The Guyana People's Militia as an auxiliary arm of the army is less conspicious in this regard, although its members are trained and also conduct exercises in the various communities along with the army. The army and the police are also used to break strikes in the sugar and bauxite industries.

The designated role of the police is that of internal security, although police are also engaged in border defense. During the last few years the police have in many respects changed their role: Police officers take the law into their own hands more often than they enforce it. Known criminals and persons wanted by the police are being shot dead, always on the pretext that they attempted to attack the police. Arrogant police boast openly about people whom they killed and are seen and heard threatening persons by saying, "Your days are numbered." Some of these police "executions" occur openly in public view. Others are alleged to occur while a detained person is in police custody. Hardly any effort is made by the police to maim or wound a felon. Invariably their aim is deadly. Rumors have it that there is a death squad in the police force and that it operates using a "hit list" of known criminals and deviants. This, of course, is a dangerous and threatening development; in the minds of most Guyanese, the police will not hesitate to kill anyone. The police have also been using unlawful and crude tactics in seeking to control the rapid growth of the underground economy and have in a short while earned a public reputation of being a corrupt law unto themselves.

The most natural and fundamental fear of the Guyanese regime is that of armed overthrow. The problem of internal security has been narrowed to an issue of regime preservation. Fears of armed overthrow are very much justified. Between December 24, 1968, and January 1969 a group of wealthy white cattle ranchers in the Rupununi region of the country (seemingly aided and abetted by Venezuelans) encouraged secession of that region of Guyana by organizing an uprising using the indigenous Amerindian people, many of whom worked for the ranchers. The secessionists took over the district's administrative office, captured the police station, and killed or injured several officials and residents in the process. The army and police responded readily and competently put down the uprising but not before the organizers fled across the borders to Venezuela. Several of the Amerindian rebels were, however, captured. A few lost their lives or were injured. The sovereignty of the state of Guyana was restored.

Toward the end of 1983 a group of Guyanese conspirators belonging to a right-wing organization called the Guyana Conservative Party was arrested in the United States and brought before a court in Cleveland, Ohio for allegedly seeking to export a cache of arms to Guyana with the aim of removing the Burnham government and assassinating its leaders. According to the late president Burnham in a 1984 address to the nation: "One of the principal witnesses for the prosecution, Mr. Courtesi, admitted that he knew that they, the plotters, had established contacts with the United States Administration." The president stated further:

> *The Caribbean Times*, a rag which issues out of Canada, editorializing on January 6, 1984 said, "This year [1984] could be the year that Forbes Burnham's nightmares of being deposed violently in Guyana come true, as Maurice Bishop was in Grenada last year.... Guyana has serious problems and very soon something will have to be done.... Guyana is in the United States backyard and ripe for plucking." We have always been cast in the role of an exotic fruit. First, we were not "ripe for independence," now, we are "ripe for plucking." But let me tell them: This is Guyana not Grenada. This is the Cooperative Republic of Guyana led by Linden Forbes Sampson Burnham.... The removal of Forbes Burnham, even if it is achieved, will profit the reactionaries and the obscurantist nothing. For if I should go, there are others, younger and more hardened who will come forward to take my place. Shooting me is a waste, another Rasta gwine take me place. You can't kill a people's movement. (Burnham 1984:3-4)

Burnham saw the policies of his government, such as nationalization and free education from kindergarten to university, as the reason imperialist powers wanted the removal of his government, which was "serious about economic and socialist democracy." The Guyana Revolution, he argued, was seen as "virulent, contagious, and infectious which had to be eradicated." The Guyana Revolution, he claimed, is aimed at achieving "socialism in our time," and because of this, it is "relentlessly and ruthlessly opposed by those who falsely believe that they were born and ordained by God to rule the lesser breed without law, those who believe that God ordered the estates of the rich and the poor nationally and internationally" (Burnham 1984:16).

President Burnham was not only concerned with the right-wing attempt to unseat his government but more particularly was worried about the perceived involvement of the U.S. administration. In an address to the Fifth Biennial Congress of his PNC party in August 1983, he criticized the United States for blocking an Inter-American Development Loan for the Abary II project:

> The present U.S. administration, as a matter of theology and ideology, disagrees violently with our economic policies generally, and would have them "corrected." We are not free to pursue our own road to development. We do not have the right Comrades to make our own policy deci-

sions. This is not mere meddling in our internal affairs, it is dictation. We must conform or else (Burnham 1983:20).

Burnham, in the same speech, went on to point to some of the efforts to destablize his government:

Devious and macabre are the tactics and the intrigues of those who would recolonise us. No holds are barred. For instance, one foreign embassy keeps an up-to-date list of foreign guests at our hotels, and depending on the purpose of their visit invite and brainwash them with anti-Guyana propaganda. One ambassador like Nicodemus, travels by night seeking to subvert senior civil servants, corporation managers, businessmen, churchmen, and even appeal court judges. The same one plies representatives of international finance institutions and friendly governments, with arguments to the effect that their first position should be that no loans should be granted to Guyana or be made available to Guyana; second position, if any loans are made available, they must be made available to the local private sector only. The express and expressed objectives are that our economy would collapse completely, confusion and disorder would follow, and from the ashes a man more "acceptable" to the powers that be would emerge, a Quisling who would pawn Guyana to the new colonisers (Burnham 1983:21).

The PNC leader saw economic destablization as one of the tactics being used to unseat his government and called on his party

to identify the enemy and his agents [for that] is the first prerequisite, to remark his tactics, the second. To plan carefully to match, outmatch, and so defeat him is the third. Let us all note, especially let the trade unions note, let the trade unionists note, that the Trade Union Movement has been selected as the prime target for subversion (Burnham 1984:21).

Forbes Burnham saw the opposition Working People's Alliance (WPA) political party as being part of the strategy of destablization.

The hope of the disloyal opposition is to infiltrate, with the assistance of a foreign power, the Trade Union Movement for its own nefarious purposes. The formula is simple—agitate for the impossible including foreign substitutes for local commodities, commit acts of sabotage, adopt a number of petit bourgeois stances, and create disaffection (Burnham 1983:21).

The government was beginning to see enemies everywhere, from without and from within. Developments within the hemisphere heightened the fears of the regime. These included the overthrow and murder of Maurice Bishop and the subsequent U.S. invasion of Grenada; the CIA's "open" covert efforts to destabilize Nicaragua and general CIA activities in Central America; and the military coup in Suriname. Things were getting too hot and too close for comfort. The PNC government was somewhat fortunate in that the main and loyal opposition, the People's Progressive Party (PPP), also professed socialism and was strongly against U.S. involvement in the affairs of an independent Guyana. The PPP, along with the WPA, joined with the PNC in a rare show of unity in condemning the U.S. invasion of Grenada. All the political parties in Guyana, including the right-wing United Force, were in support of the government in resisting the Venezuelan territorial claims. The government was fortunate in being able to count on some measure of opposition support against the United States. Most importantly, it needed to be able to count on its military to ferret out its enemies and to be loyal.

The paranoia of power has enveloped the leaders of the regime, which harbors fears of its own military apparatus. The military is constantly monitored to detect signs of any growing threat. In April 1970 the Trinidad/Tobago regiment mutinied under two young officers, Rafique Shah and Rex LaSalle. Military coups were occuring in the Third World, especially in Africa and Latin America. The PNC leadership moved swiftly to avert any such happening in Guyana. Army cadets were no longer sent for training in Britain but were trained locally instead. The activities of the army were carefully monitored by the party. Forbes Burnham defined the role of the army and demanded loyalty "from top down." Some top officers were weeded out of the army or sent back to civilian jobs. Younger officers loyal to the regime were promoted, and since then various strategies have been devised to continuously cream off the top of the Guyana Defense Force so as to facilitate upward mobility within it.

Such shuffling of the hierarchy does not occur as much in the other military institutions, but the politicians seek to ensure that party faithfuls are promoted to top positions. The loyalty of the military was essential if it were to be expected to respond to the government's demands for internal security. There are the occasional "acts of disloyalty" among officers in the military, and these are dealt with swiftly and quietly. One such incident involved a former GDF officer named Major Thomas Sattaur who was allegedly attempting to overthrow the government and, among other things, trying to recruit his own army. Further, arms and ammunition reportedly disappeared from army encampments during 1980, and this development was cause for much concern. Apart from such happenings, which are infrequent, and occasional rumors, the military in Guyana so far has been loyal to and supportive of the regime.

People have been openly calling on the army to remove the government. One opposition newspaper, *Day Clean*, has been calling on its readers to "buy a paper and give a soldier" (buy copies of *Day Clean* and give them to soldiers to read). The members of the armed forces and their families are themselves affected by the strangling economic crisis in the society. In order to avoid disaffection the government has boosted the salaries and allowances of the armed forces, and military personnel are on the average better paid than civilians; every effort is made to make things comfortable for military personnel. Nonetheless, declining economic and social conditions have resulted in the armed forces' involvement in crime, corruption, and the underground economy, both at individual and organizational levels. Military personnel themselves quietly complain about the stubborn, insensitive, and authoritarian policies of the regime.

The national security atmosphere of Guyana, both internal and external, is currently in a state of volatile calm. Externally, there are imminent threats of armed invasion, and internally, there loom possibilities of large-scale social unrest and probable armed overthrow. In all of this the national security of the country is being seriously and fundamentally threatened. The military in Guyana is at the crossroads of the internal and external demands for national security; it is not up to the external threats, and military personnel are very unhappy with some of the demands of internal security. The possibilities are that, if such circumstances remain unchanged much longer, they may want to redefine situations for themselves.

Implications for the Region

Currently, Guyana has the only undemocratic regime in the Commonwealth Caribbean. The country's embrace of militarization and its leaders' approach to problems of national security are both indicative of the unfree nature of the society. Problems of internal security result primarily from government by coercion and repression rather than government by legitimacy and consensus. Problems of external security are illustrative of the vulnerability of a small, independent, and underdeveloped nation seeking to maintain its sovereignty in a world plagued by international conflicts and power rivalries. Only Belize is similarily threatened by a more powerful neighbor, Guatamala, although Trinidad/Tobago has received its share of territorial threats from Venezuela as well.

British colonization has left, in addition to a legacy of underdevelopment, a legacy of territorial conflicts (Guyana, Belize) and a legacy of weakness (all Commonwealth Caribbean nation-states). The halo of the military strength of the British Empire was lifted with the granting of political independence. Britain can no longer be relied upon to come to the rescue of any Caribbean country faced with invasion. The Grenada invasion by the United States took place despite Britain's objections. The reality of world politics dictates the formation and institutionalization of a regional military defense grouping with each country pledging a pact of "one for all and all for one." Just as there is in the Commonwealth Caribbean regional economic and sociocultural institutions, so, too, the maturing of these new nations requires the formation and fostering of a common regional military institution pledged to the defense of all its members. With the region lacking the necessary military hardware and know-how, the creation and maintenance of such a military force should be welcomed by friendly countries.

West Indian leadership has a tradition of divisiveness, idealism, and naïveté when it comes to international politics and regional cooperation. To think that small nation-states with few resources can remain independent of meaningful political, economic, and social alliances and survive is to be not only idealistic, but also naïve. The two major superpowers have keen interests in the strategic control of the region. The Soviet Union aims to encourage the spread of socialist-oriented revolutions, and the United States aims to keep its "backyard" under its ideological, economic, and hegemonic control. Both systems, along with some of their allies and satellites, have been actively encouraging the increasing militarization of countries in the region over which they have influence and/or control in order to resist incursions of competing external forces. Arms, ammunition, military equipment, and machinery have been donated and sold to countries in the region by the superpowers. Military aid in the form of training and intelligence sharing are being fostered. The invasion of Grenada and the organization of a regional armed force for Jamaica and Eastern Caribbean countries are some of the more recent competitive involvements of a major superpower.

The invasion of Grenada thrust the regional military into the national, regional, and international limelight. The growing militarization among Caribbean countries is a function of factors internal to its various societies and factors external to these societies and the region in general. The superpowers are involved in escalating the arms race, and there is an emergent international trend whereby more-privileged countries give military aid of one sort or another to less-privileged countries. In a world that is frantically arming itself (for a third world war?), it has become much easier for struggling, underdeveloped countries to obtain guns rather than grain and arms rather than alms. The nations of the world all subscribe to a common ideology of national security, which in more and more areas is being extended to a concept of regional security. Increasingly, regional security is considered a safeguard for national security; thus, national security can only be guaranteed by increasing militarization. For instance, the United States has been pushing Japan to bolster its defenses and pushing countries of the North Atlantic Treaty Organization (NATO) to shoulder more military responsibilities.

In the Caribbean a similar strategy is being urged for the little island nation-states in the Eastern Caribbean. Such a strategy finds ready acceptance by regional governments whose domestic circumstances make them anxious to demonstrate some achievement even though it be larger armies and more guns rather than genuine economic growth and well-being. An immediate consequence of increasing militarization in countries in the region, as exemplified by Guyana, has been the frustration of the thrust toward democratization. Governments are acting with armed arrogance and are displaying increasing irritation and intolerance with any form of opposition whatsoever. Further, the increasing militarization is giving preeminence to the role and the functioning of the military and paramilitary institutions and their personnel. This increases the possibilities of coups and certainly results in the creation of a new elite among the emergent ruling classes in the region. Militarization is also being advanced at the expense of programs and policies that promote national development and well-being.

Insofar as individual CARICOM countries engage in separate military build-ups, militarization is bound to have negative effects on the economies and democratic processes of those countries and on the region as a whole. It is unlikely that any of these countries, regardless of their military strength, will be able to withstand any serious and sustained external threat. A regional strategy of defense becomes not only necessary, but imperative. CARICOM leaders and their peoples must as a matter of urgency upgrade regional cooperation to include a military treaty and a regional security force. Such a military treaty and any institutions emerging therefrom should have as their mandate the defense of the region and countries therein, rather than the defense of an ideology or the execution of selfish strategic policies of one or the other superpower. Such a military treaty must also pledge that a regional military ought never to be used against the peoples of the region. Military cooperation, even more than economic cooperation, is a formidable assurance of togetherness and support. The countries in the region can look forward to further rivalry and fragmentation of the regional movement if such a course is not followed. Militarization is not necessarily an evil. It is also a guarantee of peace and progress, or, peace for progress. Guyana's minister of foreign affairs, Rashleigh Jackson, said, "The Caribbean must be made a zone of peace" (Jackson 1982:31). A zone of peace must be a zone of cooperation, and it cannot be assured without adequate military safeguards.

Notes

1. President Ronald Reagan, for instance, in an address to the U.S. people on Central America, May 1984, saw internal strife in El Salvador and the spread of communism in the region as threats to U.S. national security.

2. The SSU was set up on February 20, 1964. It was formed by the governor after recognition of the limitations of the police force and the British Guiana Volunteer Force in coping with the upsurge of civil unrest and political violence brought about by racial struggles between the two major ethnic groups, the East Indians and the blacks. The SSU was commanded by police officers and had a strength of 500 personnel comprising equal numbers of blacks and East Indians.

3. The University of Guyana, in contrast, was allocated less than G $12 million (U.S. $2,666,666) for 1984.

4. The Special Branch of the Police, which also controls immigration, is perhaps the best-known intelligence agency in the country. Although it falls within the organizational parameters of the police force, the Special Branch is largely independent of the police, and the branch's head reports directly to the president. This agency also monitors the activities of opposition political groups and dissident individuals in the society. Keeping an eye on the military is part of its functions. The army also maintains its own intelligence arm. The PNC party uses its activists to inform on activities in the various communities and in this sense operates its own intelligence agency. The party also uses political cadres in all branches of the armed forces both to indoctrinate and to keep their ears to the ground. There are then several agencies for watching the military and for watching the watchers.

5. It is felt in some quarters that Venezuela was encouraged by a Western power to pursue its claim when there was a possibility that Guyana might gain independence under the Marxist-Leninist premier Cheddi Jagan and his People's Progressive Party government and become, like Cuba, another Soviet satellite in the hemisphere.

6. In elections held December 9, 1985, the PNC was reelected with 79 percent of the popular votes. Its nearest rival, the People's Progressive Party, was credited with 16 percent of the votes. The election results are widely viewed with skepticism. President Desmond Hoyte calls himself a true "Burnhamite" and says there will be no deviations from the course of the past twenty-two years, which, he boasts, has brought "uninterrupted peace" (Jenkins 1986:6).

7. Although the military in Guyana has been cast in the role of promoting economic development and in fact is involved in a variety of economic ventures (farming, mining, commerce), there is no evidence that these ventures are consistently profitable. There also is no adequate system of public accountability for the economic involvement of the military. The GDF engages primarily in farming but converts most of its produce for its own use. In 1980 a sum of G $2,000,000 (U.S. $444,444) appeared in the national budget as "appropriations in aid" for the GDF. In 1981 the sum was G $1,500,000 (U.S. $333,333) and in 1982, a sum of G $6,000,000 (U.S. $1,333,333). Prior to 1980 and since 1982, no "appropriations in aid" were found in the national budget.

The term "appropriations in aid" was defined as "receipts realised by departments in the course of their duties and are applied in aid of their votes." These receipts reduced the amounts budgeted for the GDF, but, invariably, supplementary provisions are sought and obtained annually for the army.

No appropriations in aid appear for the Guyana National Service, which is cited in the national budget under capital expenditure. The GNS is involved in a wider range of economic activities than the army and relative to the sums invested in it is yet to show that its farm or consumer cooperative ventures are consistently profitable.

As a part-time military body, the People's Militia is not knowingly involved in economic activities. The National Guard is as yet an unknown entity, although there are some indications of its potential for realizing revenue through its guard service. In sum, then, the military in Guyana are yet to demonstrate their viability as productive mechanisms. The national security aspect of their role predominates, and their economic involvement amounts to little more than an effort to keep them busy, albeit unprofitably so.

7

The Central American Crisis and Its Impact on Belize

Alma H. Young

Situated on the Central American mainland below Mexico and facing the Caribbean, Belize has characterized itself during the past two decades as a bridge between Central America and the Commonwealth Caribbean. Yet its links with both regions have not been fully developed. Relations with Central America have been hampered by Guatemala's controversial claim to the territory of Belize, while isolation and distance have limited closer ties between Belize and the Caribbean. Belize's ties to the United States are becoming stronger, in part because Belize is the Central American nation closest to both the United States and Cuba. Because of its strategic location, Belize has been quickly overwhelmed by regional events outside its control.

The country developed from the pirate and smuggler settlements that grew up among the secluded bays of the uninhabited coast. By 1638 the British settlement had become a major provider of logwood and mahogany. However, the country did not become a British colony until 1862; by then the traditional basis of the settlement as an English-speaking, timber-producing enclave already was eroding as a result of the immigration of an agricultural population of Indian and Spanish-speaking refugees from neighboring Yucatán (Waddell 1982:5). By the time Belize became an independent nation within the Commonwealth in 1981, its population of 155,000 had characteristics that would link it to the Caribbean and to Central America. The two largest ethnic groups in this culturally varied society are black Creoles (40 percent) of West Indian heritage, and Spanish-speaking Mestizos (33 percent), who are close to Mexico culturally and geographically.

Although Belize has not been drawn overtly into the violence that is raging throughout the area, the escalating crisis in Central America reminds Belize that it cannot escape its geographical boundaries. Thousands of refugees now pour across the Belizean borders. Millions of dollars in U.S. economic and military aid have become available to help "stabilize" Belize, and there is an increase in the military's presence in the country. The original impetus for military activity (as is discussed later in this chapter) was the need for external defense to counter the Guatemalan claim. More recently, at U.S. urging, the military has been used for internal security—mainly to stem drug trafficking. The United States encourages the military presence also as a way of ensuring that Belize will not become another battleground for control of Central America. The growth in U.S. military sales and aid to Belize as well as the growth in the Belize budget for military expenditures are examined in the following pages, and how the military presence has affected the country's internal dynamics is discussed.

The Central American Crisis

According to Wiarda, Anderson, and others, the crisis in Central America stems from a lack of responsiveness by the regimes in power in the face of contracting economic growth.[1] Problems that had been successfully masked for decades were exacerbated by the rapid social changes that occurred between the 1930s and 1960s. As a result of modernization new social and political groups emerged. Their demands for participation were, for the most part, successfully managed, due largely to economic growth at 5-7 percent annually throughout Central America.

By the 1970s, however, the process of accommodation no longer worked. The growing economic crisis, characterized by huge trade imbalances, suffocating debt, and intolerable unemployment, signaled that the economic pie could no longer expand to accommodate new groups and new demands. In such a context of contraction some groups went without. Instead of accommodation came repressive regimes that brutally closed off opportunities for further change and monopolized resources for a favorite few. This lack of responsiveness came at a time of mass-based challenge to the system and when awareness of political and economic inequities was widespread (Wiarda 1984:12-18). The resulting competition led to violence and civil war, which is now rampant throughout Central America. A broadly based revolution in Nicaragua overthrew Anastasio Somoza Debayle and his family in July 1979. Military conflict between the governing Sandinistas and the contras, aided by the United States, continues. Civil war erupted in El Salvador late in 1979 and has continued unabated. Political violence from all quarters picked up in Guatemala during approximately the same time. Honduras has become, through U.S. promotion, a base for counterrevolution against the Sandinistas in Nicaragua and the guerrilla forces in El Salvador and Guatemala.

The process of modernization and the underdevelopment that has followed, along with the political violence that is now endemic, have not been the making of Central Americans alone. Instrumental to this whole process has been the United States, through its development assistance programs, foreign investments, and military and security aid. By calling for the development of the region through industrialization, the U.S. government made it profitable for U.S. transnational corporations to invest. A new bourgeoisie tied to U.S. corporations was established. Instead of industrial development for the area, Central Americans suffered disinvestment.

Any hope of significant social change was stymied. The industrialization process left the large landholdings intact, while 40-70 percent of the rural population remained either landless or lived on tracts too small even for subsistence. This skewed land distribution contributes to inequities in income distribution that give 3 percent of the population 50 percent of the income (Barry, Wood, and Preusch 1982:6). Mechanized agriculture has contributed to the expansion of agroexport crop production, forcing many peasants off the land and into the cities to search for work. Yet, many who migrate to the cities cannot find work; unemployment and underemployment are on the rise.

While the economy has grown more and more slowly since the 1960s, inflation has skyrocketed. Costa Rica, for instance, which experienced little or no inflation in the 1960s, faced a 48 percent inflation rate in 1981. At the same time, U.S. economic aid to Central America increased fivefold between 1978 and 1982, from $86.9 million to $445.6 million (Barry, Wood, and Preusch 1982:8). In 1985 the figure stood at $780 million (U.S. Dept. of State, 1985b:335). The United States has promoted trade and investment as a way to develop Central America. In the United States the trade relationship has been extremely profitable: In 1981 the United States had a $759 million trade surplus with Central America. Central America, on the other hand, has had a steadily growing trade deficit, from $369 million in 1970 to $2.6 billion in 1980 (Barry, Wood, and Preusch 1982:10). Thus, Central American countries suffer from a severe balance-of-payments problem (see Table 7.1). In recent years, Central America's external public debt has swelled to unmanageable proportions. In 1960 the external public debt was only 3 percent of the region's national product, but by 1970 it had risen to 8 percent, and by 1980 to 46 percent(Barry, Wood, and Preusch 1982:11). In 1983 the external public debt of Central America totaled almost $11 billion, more than the value of the region's annual exports (Weeks 1985:58). Thus, instead of development, the region has experienced greater dependency.

Table 7.1

Trade and Balance of Payments Indicators
For Central America, 1979–1983
(millions of U.S. dollars)

	1979	1980	1981	1982	1983
Exports[1]	4,685	4,896	4,384	3,849	3,758
Imports[1]	4,773	5,490	5,358	4,281	4,166
Trade balance	−88	−594	−974	−432	−408
Change in reserves[2]	+160	+366	+266	−182	−230
Debt service[3]	612	780	782	730	982
Foreign debt	5,398	6,804	8,444	9,815	11,896

[1] Merchandise only

[2] Year-end change in foreign-exchange holdings

[3] Interest and amortization. Does not include for Costa Rica $263 million in 1981 and $383 million in 1982 that were part of scheduled debt service but not paid.

Source: Weeks (1985:58).

Another area in which dependency on the United States has been fostered is in military aid to Central America. The United States has regularly supplied Central America with military weapons and equipment as well as with training for military personnel. The U.S. technical and political training of the foreign military has increased the power and effectiveness of military institutions, making them powerful actors in domestic political affairs throughout the region.[2] After the fall of Somoza the United States began to pour even more military aid into the region. From 1953 to 1979, the United States spent, on the average, $5.0 million annually on the Central American military. In 1980 U.S. military aid increased to $8.8 million, in 1981 to $44.8 million, and in 1982 to $109.1 million (Barry, Wood, and Preusch 1982:9). In 1985 the United States allocated $236 million on the Central American military (U.S. Dept. of State, 1985b:345).

The priority accorded security in the Reagan administration's foreign policy is apparent in the emphases given to particular programs, regions, and countries. Military aid is favored over economic aid. Security-oriented economic aid is preferred over development assistance. Aid is also heavily concentrated in countries where U.S. political and strategic interests are perceived to be threatened by the Soviet Union or its proxies (Sewell, Feinberg, and Kallab 1985:98). Thus, in Central America, the part of the world that the U.S. State Department has said presents "the main challenge to U.S. interests," development assistance increased by 80 percent between 1980 and 1983, but security assistance grew by 2,845 percent between 1980 and 1983 (see Table 7.2). Security assistance therefore is being used to bolster stability in Central America, and in the process military personnel and their allies gain a stronger foothold in the society, and the conflict escalates.

The role being played by the United States in providing security assistance in Central America is also being adopted by the United States in the Eastern Caribbean. Security assistance to the Eastern Caribbean increased from $4 million in 1980 to $13.3 million in 1983 and to approximately $25 million in 1985. The increase is even more dramatic when we take into account the fact that many of these countries did not even have armies and thus received no U.S. military aid before 1979. As Marlene Dixon has argued, U.S. actions in the Caribbean and in Central America signal a search for a new foreign policy, one based on aggressive militarism (Dixon 1985:ix).

The fight for a future foreign policy has taken its most definitive shape regarding U.S. policy toward Central America and the Caribbean. According to the new right ideologues, President Carter "lost" Nicaragua to "communism," and the United States had to reassert worldwide superiority over the Soviet Union and reject détente with its surrogates, Cuba and Nicaragua. Recent policy reports all justify the long-term militarization of Central America and the Caribbean.[3] These countries are viewed as "threatened" and thus have received large amounts of economic and military assistance. The English-speaking Caribbean, particularly those countries in the Eastern Caribbean, are viewed as a major security risk, due in part to the departure of Great Britain from the region. Thus, as has been argued, the United States has stepped in to fill the military void left by Great Britain and protect its interests by promoting the militarization of these societies (Beruff 1985:74).

Table 7.2

Changes in the Regional Emphasis of U.S. Bilateral Aid
($ millions current)

Development Assistance[a]			
Region	1977-1980 Average	1983	Percentage Change
Sub-Saharan Africa	397.0	518.4	+31
Middle East and N. Africa[b]	117.3	141.5	+21
Israel and Egypt	193.0	255.1	+32
East Asia	395.2	237.3	−40
South Asia	527.5	559.4	+ 6
South America	151.0	194.7	+29
Central America[d]	232.5	417.8	+80
Other	56.8	38.0	−33
Security Assistance[c]			
Region	1977-1980 Average	1983	Percentage Change
Sub-Saharan Africa	137.8	402.9	+ 192.0
Middle East and N. Africa[b]	602.9	1,147.1	+ 90.0
Israel and Egypt	3,685.4	4,561.9	+ 2.4
East Asia	364.1	422.5	+ 16.0
South Asia	1.0	461.3	+4,603.0
South America	34.5	10.2	− 70.0
Central America[d]	21.7	639.1	+2,845.0
Other	450.5	827.1	+ 84.0

[a] Development assistance includes bilateral development assistance, P.L. 480, and other bilateral development programs.

[b] Excludes Israel and Egypt.

[c] Security assistance includes all military assistance programs and the Economic Support Fund. Interregional programs are excluded.

[d] Includes Central America, the Caribbean, and Mexico.

Source: Sewell, Feinberg, and Kallab (1985:98).

U.S. actions in the last several years have most clearly defined the region as the American Mediterranean. The region is now called the Caribbean Basin, thereby including those countries in the Caribbean as well as those on the Caribbean (including Central America), and thus more succintly naming the U.S. sphere of influence. Given the region's cultural and socioeconomic diversity, only Washington's geopolitical concerns define the Caribbean as a coherent unity. As defined by Secretary of State George Shultz, the stakes in the region include the fact that

> the Caribbean is an unfenced neighborhood that we share with 27 island and coastal nations... a vital strategic and commercial artery for the United States.... If the region should become prey to social and economic upheaval, and dominated by regimes hostile to us, the consequences for our security would be immediate and far-reaching (quoted in "A Lovely Piece..." 1984:19).

The familiar strategic rationale for U.S. involvement in Central America is now being applied to the Caribbean as a whole as the area is drawn more tightly into the U.S. security zone. Belize's role in this redefinition of the area is worth considering.

Change Comes to "Peaceful" Belize

When addressing the nation on September 21, 1982, on the occasion of its first anniversary of independence from Great Britain, former prime minister George Price declared that Belize is struggling to maintain a "climate of peace," which distinguishes it from its neighbors.[4] Belize has not been drawn overtly into the violence raging throughout the area, and the country also is set apart from its neighbors in other significant ways. The British influence and the majority black population have oriented Belize more to the Caribbean economic and political community. Historically, the Caribbean, especially the English-speaking Caribbean, has been immune from the political extremism and authoritarian and violent politics that have characterized Central America. However, the March 1979 coup in Grenada, followed by the 1980 coup in Suriname and the 1983 implosion in Grenada, and the proclivity being shown by several Caribbean states (including Guyana, Dominica, St. Lucia, St. Vincent, and Jamaica) toward authoritarianism and political violence has led one scholar to speak of the "Central Americanization of the English-speaking Caribbean" (Erisman 1983). Why the change in orientation in the Caribbean? Some speculate that it is the result of these countries being drawn into the East-West conflict.[5] Others suggest that greater internal repression becomes necessary because past safety valves are ineffective in dissipating popular protest of current economic hardships.[6]

Although Belize cannot yet be characterized as a violent or militarized society, the escalating crisis in Central America is impacting Belize in a number of ways. Salvadoran, Honduran, and Guatemalan refugees now pour over its borders. Of greater concern are the occasional Guatemalan troop maneuvers along the Belize border. Belizeans fear Guatemala will attempt to seize the country, for Guatemala has refused to recognize Belize's independence and maintains a one hundred-year-old dispute with Britain regarding possession of the territory.[7] The greater the degree of conflict within Guatemala, the stronger the claim tends to be pressed. However, the clearest signal that the crisis is impacting Belize is that the country is being drawn more tightly to the United States—that is, Belize is falling more firmly within the U.S. orbit. The United States has moved in quickly to replace British influence in Belize through economic assistance, aid for private investment, and military assistance.

In the 1984 general elections the People's United Party (PUP), which had led the country for thirty years, lost to the relatively new United Democratic Party (UDP) (see Pitt 1984). The People's United Party was the nationalist party of the 1950s that successfully brought into the economic and political mainstream the largely disenfranchised Mestizos and Indians found mainly in the rural areas. In the process the PUP helped to unify the disparate parts of the country. During the years the PUP became the voice of labor, farmers, peasants—those Price called "the little man." Traditionally, the opposition, most recently in the guise of the United Democratic Party, has been the party of civil servants, Belize City Creoles, and colonial interests. Although decidedly a minority party until recently, the opposition was able for almost twenty years to counter the PUP's attempts to gain independence for Belize.[8] The party began to lose its minority status as the economy began to fade, especially in the sugar industry that dominates the Mestizo north, and the unions lost their grip on their members. Many turned to the UDP in the search for economic recovery. The UDP, which campaigned for increased foreign capital, especially private investment from the United States, and had less nationalistic fervor than the PUP, was ready to receive U.S. aid of all kinds. UDP leaders were especially eager to be courted by the United States at a time when Britain was trying to extricate itself from Belize and thus from the Central American crisis.

Another reason that the PUP lost the elections was the split within the party's leadership, exacerbated by the availability of funds from the United States, between the right wing, which is strongly pro-U.S., and the left wing, which favors a more broadly based economic and foreign policy. The membership of the two wings is quite distinct. The left wingers are younger, having entered politics in the late 1960s and early 1970s upon their return from university training abroad. Because of their professional backgrounds they might be considered technocrats, and it was from that vantage that they attempted to run their ministries. This was in stark contrast to members of the right wing, most of whom had been with the party since the late 1950s and early 1960s and were heavily involved in patronage politics. The left wingers had been exposed to the nonaligned movement while studying abroad and embraced its message. The party used the left wingers' nonaligned orientation to rally Third World support for Belize's territorial integrity in the face of Guatemala's claim to the country. The strategy worked, and Belize gained its independence—the Third World effectively countered Guatemala's saber-rattling. Belize's political factions, however, continued to grow further apart after independence.

Conducting business became much more difficult for a government torn into factions. Price tried to moderate between the two groups, but his efforts were not enough to keep charges and countercharges from being aired in the press and in public. The UDP government is expected to have no such problems regarding foreign policy, for its support of U.S. policy appears clear. The influence of the United States on Belizean politics is expected to grow.

Increased Military and Economic Aid

At the time of Belize's independence Britain agreed to maintain an eighteen hundred-troop garrison in Belize for "an appropriate period" to defend Belize against possible Guatemalan aggression. The troops plus four Harrier fighter jets are estimated to cost Britain $50 million annually (Davie 1983). British forces are rotated on a six-month basis, many coming directly from Northern Ireland. Apart from an occasional training accident the British soldiers face little danger. Their major responsibility is to patrol the Belize-Guatemala border on a regular basis. Their main camp is at the Belize International Airport in Belize City, but there are also several small encampments along the border. Their other responsibility is to help train the seven hundred-member Belize Defense Force (BDF) started in 1978. British soldiers lecture regularly at the BDF training school, and BDF officers are sent to Britain for further training. It has been government policy for British military presence to remain low key, but it is difficult to "hide" eighteen hundred soldiers within a small population. Therefore, soldiers in fatigues and personnel carriers rumbling through the streets have become common sights. On the whole, friction between the soldiers and the civilian population has been minimal.

Great Britain deliberately left vague the length of time it would defend Belize. The Thatcher government has made it known that it would like to end this arrangement in the near future. The U.S. government, on the other hand, would like for Britain to commit its troops to Belize until the Central American region is stable. The United States fears that once the British military presence has been withdrawn, Belize could become a Cuban bridgehead and thus another battleground for control of Central America. The British are wary of having their forces drawn into the Central American conflict and thus are even more anxious to leave Belize (Davie 1983). Although the Belize government has discussed possible security arrangements with Mexico, Canada, and several countries in the Commonwealth Caribbean, no suitable replacement has been found. This seems to open the door for some kind of defense agreement with the United States.

U.S. military and economic aid to Belize is increasing. In 1981 the United States spent $748,000 for Belize, all of which went to the Peace Corps. In 1982, the figure was $10.98 million, of which $10 million went for promotion of U.S. investment and trade under the Economic Support Fund (ESF) program, $26,000 for training military personnel, and $958,000 for the Peace Corps (Barry, Wood, and Preusch 1982:140). In 1986 the United States allocated $5.1 million on security assistance programs in Belize, of which $4.0 million came from the Economic Support Fund. An additional $9.3 million came from other economic assistance programs, including $6.8 million for development aid and $2.5 million for the Peace Corps (U.S. Department of State 1985b:335). The U.S. Agency for International Development established bilateral programs in Belize in January 1983, part of whose funds stemmed from allocations under the Caribbean Basin Initiative. Fourteen million dollars were allocated in 1984 and $10 million for 1985 (U.S. AID 1984). Most of these funds will be used for economic stabilization and fiscal improvement as well as to increase investment opportunities for U.S. corporations and thus to tie the region economically to the United States.

In 1981 the United States began negotiations with the government to establish an airfield and military base in Belize. Those negotiations continue. The United States is sending military advisers to train the Belizean army, and members of the BDF are receiving training at U.S. facilities in Panama. In fiscal year (FY) 1982, 25 Belizean soldiers were trained under the International Military Education and Training (IMET) program; in FY 1983 more than 60 Belizean soldiers were trained under the program (Barry, Wood, and Preusch 1982:140). In FY 1986, 100 soldiers are expected to be trained under IMET; 16 of those soldiers will be trained in the United States (U.S. Department of State 1985*b*:335). The U.S. government is also providing Belize with $1 million in sophisticated electronic equipment with military capabilities. Between 1980 and 1982 the purchase of U.S.-manufactured light arms and combat-support equipment under the Direct Commercial Sales Program more than doubled in Belize, from $217,000 to $503,000 (Barry, Wood, and Preusch 1982:142). The major items that fall into this category are police weapons and related equipment, such as tear-gas grenades.

The growth in U.S. economic and military aid for Belize and the readiness with which the Belize government has been willing to accept it, are signs of the incorporation of Belize into the U.S. sphere of economic and political influence. Belize, like the rest of the Caribbean, is firmly becoming a part of the American Mediterranean. As U.S. aid to Belize increases, it becomes more likely that Belize will become another U.S. client state in Central America. Increased U.S. influence has hampered relations between Belize and two of its allies, Cuba and Nicaragua. Nicaragua and Cuba were active and important supporters of Belizean independence, but recently relations have cooled.[9] It appears Belize will have to pick its diplomatic friends more carefully these days. There is also the fear within the country that if Belize continues to increase its military personnel and equipment, this arsenal could be used not only for national defense but also for internal security.

Internal Security

While the defense of the territorial integrity of Belize continues to be of major importance to the government, the Belize Defense Force is not restricted to a military role. The BDF is expected to assist the police in the maintenance of law and order. To that end, the BDF is assisting the Belize Police Force in its campaign to stop the drug trafficking that has reached major proportions in Belize.

Under pressure from the United States, the Belize government has sought to stem the illegal cultivation of marijuana. Not only have the security forces been going through the dense jungle on search-and-destroy missions, they are now using chemical warfare (paraquat spray). With the assistance of the U.S. Drug Enforcement Agency and the Mexican government, the Belize government began the spraying of fields in 1982 and continued in 1983. The offensive was discontinued during 1984 because of the general elections, but plans are under way to resume the spraying. As a result of the earlier spraying, more than three thousand plantations covering an area of 14,400 acres were destroyed. There have been an increasing number of arrests and convictions for marijuana cultivation. Drug laws also have been stiffened, including for the first time in Belizean history the provision for trials without juries (*The New Belize* 1983:86).

The use of paraquat spray caused quite a protest throughout the country from environmentalists, farmers, and others. Critics charged that the spraying was done to appease the United States because Caribbean Basin Initiative rules stipulate that the United States may withhold aid to those countries that do not do the maximum to stamp out the drug trade. When the Belize government discontinued the spraying in 1983 in preparation for the general elections, U.S. officials were said to be quite annoyed for they felt that Belize was not doing enough to halt the drug trafficking in the country (see Brinkley 1985). The Belize government responded by increasing search-and-destroy missions by the police and the army. The discontent in the north, where most of the marijuana fields are located, was significant. As some put it, the Belize government was destroying people's livelihoods because the United States dictated such destruction. The PUP government's handling of the drug problem is seen as another of the reasons for the party's loss of the 1984 general elections (Young, forthcoming). Ironically, the new Esquivel government is expected to be more cooperative in assisting the United States in its campaign against the drug trade.[10]

The United States recently stepped up its antidrug campaign. In 1984 the U.S. government busted a cocaine smuggling ring that moved the drug from Colombia to Miami through the Belize International Airport. U.S. officials are trying to extradite two Belizeans, an assistant superintendent of police and the manager of the international airport, for their alleged participation in the cocaine smuggling ring. The PUP government established a one-person Commission of Inquiry to investigate the allegations;

the commission has yet to report its findings (*Amandala* 1984). In April 1985 a former minister of government from the north of Belize was arrested in Miami for conspiracy to supply 5,000 pounds of marijuana a month to the United States (*Amandala* 1985; Nordheimer 1985). Other Belizeans recently have been arrested in Miami on drug possession and conspiracy charges.

The crackdown on drugs may be necessary, but it is feared in some quarters that under sanction from the United States, the Belize government may use the enforcement of drug laws to become more repressive toward its citizens. The trial and conviction of two BDF soldiers in 1984 for shooting innocent citizens, one of them fatally, during a drug operation does nothing to calm the fears. Roadblocks in the north have become commonplace, as soldiers search for drugs passing through the country. Increasing numbers of citizens have lodged complaints of brutality against BDF soldiers.

Since 1978 when the Belize Defense Force was formed, there has been a steady growth in the amount of government funds devoted to defense requirements (see Table 7.3). The increase in expenditures in 1982/83 and 1983/84 occurred when the big push to stem the drug traffic was under way. Thus, it can be argued that the BDF is more concerned with internal security than external defense.

Table 7.3

Expenditures for Defense, as Percentage of Change, 1978-1984/85

	Amount	% Change
1978[a]	$1,215,530	–
1979[b]	2,293,063	+47.0
1980/81[c]	2,917,372	+21.0
1981/82[a]	2,829,234	– 3.1
1982/83[a]	4,910,918	+42.0
1983/84[c]	6,979,760	+29.6
1984/85[b]	6,961,674	– 0.2

[a] Actual expenditures
[b] Revised estimates
[c] Approved estimates
Sources: Belize House of Representatives (1977; 1980/81; 1981/82; 1982/83; 1983/84; 1984/85).

Table 7.4

Expenditures for Police, as Percentage of Change, 1976-1984/85

	Amount	% Change
1976[a]	$1,935,209	–
1977[a]	1,976,444	+ 2.1
1978[a]	2,098,085	+ 5.8
1979[b]	2,123,600	+ 1.2
1980/81[c]	2,941,332	+27.8
1981/82[a]	4,177,133	+29.6
1982/83[a]	3,451,502	−21.0
1983/84[c]	3,744,335	+ 7.8
1984/85[b]	3,475,202	− 7.7

[a] Actual expenditures
[b] Revised estimates
[c] Approved estimates

Sources: Belize House of Representatives (1976; 1980/81; 1981/82; 1982/83; 1983/84; 1984/85).

Expenditures for the police show, for the most part, a corresponding steady growth (see Table 7.4). In preparation for independence (1980 and 1981), when the country was known to be divided on the issue of independence, and immediately after independence, there were significant increases in expenditures for the police. Expenditures for the military and the police also are assuming a greater proportion of the total operating budget. In 1983/84, for example, expenditures for the two security forces (the BDF and the police) amounted to $10.72 million and accounted for 10.9 percent of the operating budget. In that same year 9.6 percent of the budget, or $9.51 million, was allocated to primary and secondary education. Thus, the impact of the security forces on the country is becoming significant, whether viewed in monetary or political terms.

Refugees

The third area in which the Central American crisis is felt in Belize is the number of refugees entering the country (Everitt 1984). Central American nations, with the possible exception of El Salvador, have a significant number of legal and illegal refugees, but for Belize with its population of 155,000, the numbers are alarming. There is a feeling among Belizeans that they are being "swamped by outsiders." Officials from the Ministry of Home Affairs speak of 16,000 "illegal squatters," mainly Hondurans, Guatemalans, and Salvadorans, in addition to the 4,600 persons recognized by the U.N. High Commission for Refugees. Unofficial sources say the U.N. figure is low, but even assuming it is correct, the total of 20,600 means that for every 15 Belizeans there are 2 aliens (*Central America Report* 1984:180). It appears that Belize is being targeted as a country to receive the refugees fleeing the major economic and political upheavals sweeping the region. With its low population density Belize might appear a logical place to resettle "displaced" people. However, in the process Belize would become a "new nation" (Huyck and Bouvier 1983:53, 58). In a 1984 broadcast then home affairs minister Vernon Courtenay said the refugee situation "is unsatisfactory and poses a threat to our Belizean heritage."

Of great concern is the likely possibility that the ethnic composition of the country will change. Historically, the major ethnic group has been, and still is, black Creoles, but Mestizos are quickly gaining in number. With the influx of Central American refugees, Creoles could find their majority status eclipsed. The refugees could contribute to making the English-speaking black population more Spanish-speaking and white. The problem of the refugees coming in search of peace and a place to work is compounded by the fact that large numbers of black Belizeans have been emigrating for years to the United States, England, and Canada in search of work. In the late 1960s and early 1970s ethnicity played a significant role in Belizean politics. Through a process of cooptation and isolation, ethnic politics at the time did not reach a level of violence, although fears of loss of jobs, housing, and status ran high among many Creoles (Young 1979: 32-36). Whether more repressive measures might not be used this time if ethnicity becomes a significant political issue is a question that needs to be more fully considered.

Besides the hostility spreading because of increased competition for scarce jobs, aliens are often suspected of spreading communicable and contagious diseases. More menancing to the country, however, is the rising crime rate, much of it blamed on the aliens. The PUP government blamed the upswing in the number of brutal murders on "strangers to Belize" because most of the incidents occur in the sugar belt in the north where there is the largest concentration of Central American refugees (*The New Belize* 1984:7-9).

Many of the aliens come originally as cane cutters with valid work permits. Eventually, however, they disappear into the jungles and are joined by relatives and friends who settle illegally— many become involved in the lucrative business of marijuana cultivation in the dense jungle interior. The government alleges that these marijuana fields are often guarded by men heavily armed with automatic rifles and submachine guns.

The drug traffic, of course, has authorities most concerned. The government is moving to control the existence of airstrips, many of which are now privately owned and not registered. Planes will be forbidden to land in unauthorized places. Blocking air traffic is only part of the solution. Belize's long, uninhabited shoreline is ideal for small craft engaged in drug trafficking, and lately several boats have been caught, jammed with marijuana. In all of these operations the BDF soldiers have played a primary role. Some gun battles have ensued.

Although Belize is faced with large numbers of illegal aliens, attempts to develop permanent resettlement schemes to accommodate legal refugees in Belize continue. The Valley of Peace is a rural land resettlement scheme in the Belize River Valley involving Salvadoran refugees and Belizean families. Individual families receive 50 acres of land on a lease from the government. After the land is developed the families own it. The resettlement of the 50,000 acres earmarked for the project began in March 1982. The cost of the project is approximately $1 million and is provided by the U.N. High Commission on Refugees. The Belizean government donated the land, and the Mennonites, the religious sect that came to Belize in 1966 and is now a major agricultural producer, provided personnel and some funds (*The New Belize* 1982:6).

Under prodding from the United States, the PUP government agreed to allow Haitians to resettle in the country where the government would give them fifty acres of land and encourage them to farm. The offer is aimed at Haitians detained in the United States or Puerto Rico, not those coming directly from Haiti because the U.S. government would not pay for their resettlement (*Latin American Weekly Report* 1982). This offer is viewed as an attempt by the government to maintain the racial balance within the country. However, few Haitians have accepted this offer of resettlement. Nevertheless, the permanent resettlement villages have experienced only minimal tension between refugees and Belizean residents, and the villages appear to have been accepted by the surrounding areas. Illegal aliens, on the other hand, appear to have been much less readily accepted.

Conclusion

Compared to the turmoil throughout Central America, Price may have been correct when he called Belize "a peaceful corner" in the region. However, actions are being taken that could pull Belize closer to the conflict and to the legacy from which the conflict stems. Greater U.S. involvement in the country, increased military presence within the society, and possible overt conflict between ethnic groups could lead to an escalation of tensions within Belize that might easily spill over into violence. New groups are clamoring for greater participation in the political and economic mainstream at a time when the economy is faltering and a new party is at the helm.

One countervailing force to internal violence in Belize has been the presence of the British—now the British garrison. When violence broke out during preindependence attempts to resolve the Anglo-Guatemala dispute, the British troops moved in quickly to restore calm and order. However, once the British troops are gone, and many believe their leaving is imminent, who will maintain peace between competing factions? Some are looking to the United States.

However, peace in the Caribbean Basin is not the U.S. purpose. The role presently being played by the United States would suggest an entrenching of the status quo.[11] Through the provision of massive amounts of security assistance, the United States has provided resources to elites in power throughout the region that are often used to limit access to the political and economic center. By trying to reassert its hegemonic authority in the region through "covert" intervention (through the use of client armies), the United States has created conditions that favor an escalation of tensions, less competition between elites, and more repression. Attempts by various groups in these societies to counter the status quo have been viewed as subversive. Peaceful negotiations among competing factions have been eschewed in favor of an aggressive militarism. The geopolitical vision of a Caribbean Basin means devising uniform policies for a disparate group of states, with military containment of "communism" being the core of those policies. In Central America the U.S. government could rely on local security forces, with their long history as willing U.S. clients. In the English-speaking Caribbean, however, it means enhancing the

U.S. military presence in Caribbean waters and building a military capacity where little existed before. As Belize becomes drawn more tightly into the U.S. sphere of influence, Belize's position as a peaceful corner in Central America may be threatened. It would be a pity for such to become Belize's fate.

Notes

1. The literature on the Central American crisis is becoming quite extensive. See, for example, Wiarda (1984:12-18); Anderson (1982); Anderson (1967: especially Chapter 4); and Woodward (1976).

2. See, for example, Millett (1984); and the "Introduction" to this volume.

3. The policy reports include: Bipartisan Commission on Central America (1984); Rand Corporation (1984); and Committee of Santa Fe (1980).

4. As cited in *The New Belize* (1982:4). Price went on to discuss the dangers that Belize faces as a result of the political and economic dislocations in the region. Also see Broad (1984).

5. See the chapters in this volume by Boodhoo and Phillips.

6. See the chapters in this volume by Watson and Danns.

7. See Young (1981); and Young and Braveboy-Wagner (forthcoming).

8. See Grant (1976:102-106); and Young and Young (1983).

9. Jamail (1984b:15). At his press conference on January 9, 1985, Prime Minister Manuel Esquivel explained that Belize had to be represented at the Sandinista's sixth anniversary celebration ceremonies becaue Nicaragua had been a steadfast friend in the dispute with Guatemala, but that no high-ranking government official was sent because his government did not want to send the wrong cue to the United States.

10. At a press conference on April 24, 1985, Prime Minister Esquivel expressed the view that drug trafficking in Belize was more pernicious for the country than the chemical spraying of marijuana fields.

11. Diplomatic sources suggest that there has been a shift recently in President Reagan's foreign policy away from the strident anticommunist rhetoric of the early years toward the more pragmatic mainstream policy in which the United States leans on dictatorships of the right as well as of the left. In his March 14, 1986, message to Congress Reagan said that "the American people believe in human rights and oppose tyranny in whatever form,

whether of the left or right." Perhaps Reagan now sees that support for democracy is the best way to advance anticommunism (Saikowski 1986:1). Yet the military build-up continues in the Caribbean. As Reagan pledges his support for democracy he is campaigning for additional military aid to the contras fighting the Sandinista government in Nicaragua.

The Contributors

Ken I. Boodhoo, from Trinidad, teaches international relations at Florida International University. He formerly was associated with the Institute of International Relations at the University of the West Indies-St. Augustine, Trinidad. He is completing a manuscript on Grenada. He is the author of *Eric Williams: The Man and the Leader*.

George K. Danns, from Guyana, teaches in the Department of Sociology and is the former assistant dean of the Faculty of Social Sciences at the University of Guyana. He has been a senior Fulbright scholar at the University of Michigan. He has written widely on issues of leadership, corruption, and militarization in the Caribbean. He is the author of *Domination and Power in Guyana: A Study of the Police in a Third World Context*.

Dion E. Phillips, from Barbados, teaches in the Division of the Social Sciences of the College of the Virgin Islands. He is a research consultant with the Eastern Caribbean Center of the College of the Virgin Islands. He formerly taught sociology at Howard University. His research and writings have focused primarily on the role of the military in the Eastern Caribbean.

Betty Sedoc-Dahlberg, from Suriname, is the former dean of the Faculty of Social Science and rector magnificus at the University of Suriname. She has been a Fulbright scholar at the Massachusetts Institute of Technology. She is presently a visiting professor at the University of Florida at Gainesville. She is completing a book on development policies in Suriname.

Hilbourne A. Watson, from Barbados, teaches in the Department of Political Science at Howard University. He has written extensively on U.S. foreign policy in the Caribbean and on Caribbean migration and is currently focusing on the role of merchant capital in the Caribbean in the colonial and postcolonial period. He recently served as guest editor of *Contemporary Marxism* no. 10: "Islands of Discontent."

Alma H. Young teaches in the School of Urban and Regional Studies and is associate vice chancellor for Academic Affairs at the University of New Orleans. She is president of the Caribbean Studies Association and former editor of the *Caribbean Studies Newsletter*. Her research and writings have focused on comparative urbanization and political developments in the English-speaking Caribbean, especially in Belize.

Bibliography

Adams, Trevor (1982). "Protecting the Waters Around Us." *Sunday Sun*, February 28, 11.

Adelman, Alan, and Reid Reading, eds. (1984). *Confrontation in the Caribbean Basin: International Perspectives on Security, Sovereignty and Survival*. Pittsburgh, Pa.: Center for Latin American Studies, University of Pittsburgh.

Aglietta, Michael (1980). *A Theory of Capitalist Regulation*. London: New Left Books.

Alavi, Hamza (1976). "The State in Post-Colonial Societies: Pakistan and Bangladesh." *New Left Review* no. 94 (July-August):28-42.

Althusser, Louis (1971). *Lenin and Philosophy*. New York: Monthly Review Press.

Amandala, May 11, 1984; April 12, 1985.

Ambursley, Fitzroy, and Robin Cohen, eds. (1983). *Crisis in the Caribbean*. London: Heineman.

Amnesty International (1983). *Amnesty International Report 1983*. London: Amnesty International Publications.

Anderson, Charles W. (1967). *Politics and Economic Change in Latin America: The Governing of Restless Nations*. Princeton, N.J.: Van Nostrand.

Anderson, Perry (1977). *Considerations on Western Marxism*. London: Verso Books.

Anderson, Thomas P. (1982). *Politics in Central America: Guatemala, El Salvador, Honduras and Nicaragua*. New York: Praeger.

Baber, Colin, and Henry B. Jeffrey (1986). *Guyana: Politics, Economics and Society*. Boulder, Colo.: Lynne Reinner.

Barbados Labour Party (1976). *Barbados Labour Party Manifesto*. Bridgetown, Barbados: Barbados Labour Party.

Barbados Labour Party (1981). *Barbados Labour Party Manifesto*. Bridgetown, Barbados: Barbados Labour Party.

160

Barrow, Errol (1983). "The Danger of Rescue Operations." *Caribbean Review* 12, no. 4 (Fall):3-4.

Barry, Tom, and Deb Preusch (1986). *The Central America Fact Book.* Albuquerque, N.Mex.: The Resource Center.

Barry, Tom, Beth Wood, and Deb Preusch (1982). *Dollars and Dictators: A Guide to Central America.* Albuquerque, N.M.: The Resource Center.

Barry, Tom, Beth Wood and Deb Preusch (1984). "Caribbean Alert: The Militarization of the Region." *The Other Side of Paradise.* New York: Grove Press, pp. 196-209.

Belize House of Representatives (1975). *Estimates of Revenues and Expenditures for 1976.* Belize: Government Printery.

Belize House of Representatives (1977). *Estimates of Revenues and Expenditures for 1978.* Belize: Government Printery.

Belize House of Representatives (1980). *Estimates of Revenues and Expenditures for 1980/81.* Belize: Government Printery.

Belize House of Representatives (1981). *Estimates of Revenues and Expenditures for 1981/82.* Belize: Government Printery.

Belize House of Representatives (1982). *Estimates of Revenues and Expenditures for 1982/83.* Belize: Government Printery.

Belize House of Representatives (1983). *Estimates of Revenues and Expenditures for 1983/84.* Belize: Government Printery.

Belize House of Representatives (1984). *Estimates of Revenues and Expenditures for 1984/85.* Belize: Government Printery.

Beruff, Jorge R. (1983). "Militarization and the Caribbean Basin Initiative." *Caribbean Perspective* 2, no. 1 (Summer):17-35.

Beruff, Jorge Rodriguez (1985). "Puerto Rico and U.S. Militarization." *Contemporary Marxism*, no. 10:68-91.

Bishop, Maurice (1977). Interview. *Trinidad Express*, April 1.

Bishop, Maurice (1982a). Interview. *World Marxism Review* 25, 4 (April):63-67.

Bishop, Maurice (1982b). "Lines of March for the Party." Speech to the general meeting of the party, St. George's, Grenada. September 13. Mimeo.

Black, George (1985). "MARE NOSTRUM: U.S. Security Policy in the English-Speaking Caribbean." *NACLA/Report on the Americas* 19, no. 4 (July-August):13-48.

Blanke, B., V. Jurgens, and H. Kastendiek (1978). "On the Current Marxist Discussion on the Analysis of Form and Function of the Bourgeois State." In Holloway, John H., and Sol Picciotto, eds. *State and Capital*, London: E. Arnold.

Bolland, O. Nigel (1986). *Belize: A New Nation in Central America.* Boulder, Colo.: Westview Press.

Boodhoo, Ken I. (1986). *Eric Williams: The Man and the Leader.* Washington, D.C.: University Press of America.

Boron, A. (1979). "New Forms of Capitalist State in Latin America: An Exploration." *Race and Class* 20, no. 3 (Winter):263-276.

Bray, David (1985). "Industrialization, Employment Crisis and Labor Migration: A Comparison of Puerto Rico, Jamaica and the Dominican Republic." Paper delivered at the Ninth Annual Conference on the World-System: "Crisis in the Caribbean Basin: Past and Present," Tulane University, New Orleans, March 28-30.

Brinkley, Joel (1985). "Drug Crops Are Up in Export Nations, State Dept. Says." *New York Times,* February 15.

Broad, Dave (1984). "Belize–On the Rim of the Cauldron." *Monthly Review* 35, no. 9 (February):38-47.

Budhall, Russell, and Layne Phillips (1983). "Letters of Complaint" to Amnesty International (June). Mimeo.

Burnham, Forbes (1983). "Will to Survive." Address at the Fifth Biennial Congress of the People's National Congress, Georgetown, Guyana, August.

Burnham, Forbes (1984). "Let Us Use Our Resources." Address on the occasion of the fourteenth anniversary of the republic, Georgetown, Guyana, February 23.

C47:Vijf en Twintig Jaren Strijd (C47: Twenty-five Years of Struggle) (1984). Paramaribo: C47 Labor Federation.

Caribbean Contact (Barbados), November 1980; September 1982; March 1984; October 1985.

Central American Report, June 15, 1984.

The Committee of Santa Fe, Lewis Tambs, ed. (1980). *A New Inter-American Policy for the Eighties.* Washington, D.C.: Council for Inter-American Security.

Consortium of Labor Federations (1984). *"Grondgedechte met betrekking tot de Structurering van de Nieuwe Democracie"* ("Basic thoughts Concerning the Structuring of the New Democracy"). Paramaribo, (April). Mimeo.

Danns, George K. (1978). "Militarization and Development: An Experiment in Nation-Building." *Transition* 1, no. 1 (April):23-44.

Danns, George K. (1982). *Domination and Power in Guyana: A Study of the Police in a Third World Context.* New Brunswick, N.J.: Transition Books.

Danns, George K. (1984). "The Role of the Military in the National Security of Guyana." Paper presented at the Ninth Annual Meeting of the Caribbean Studies Association, St. Kitts, May 30-June 2.

Davie, John (1983). "Under the Volcano." *London Times,* October 2.

Day Clean (Guyana), April 11, 1980.

Decalo, Samuel (1976). *Coups and Army Rule in Africa: Studies in Military Style.* New Haven, Conn.: Yale University Press.

"The Declaration of St. George's–Towards One Caribbean" (1979). *Bulletin of Eastern Caribbean Affairs* 5, no. 3 (July-August):18, 20-21.

De Ware Tijd (Paramaribo), November 20, 1982.

Dew, Edward (1976). *The Difficult Flowering of Suriname: Ethnicity and Politics in a Plural Society.* The Hague: Mouton.

Diederich, Bernard (1984). "The End of West Indian Innocence: Arming the Police." *Caribbean Review* 13, no. 2 (Spring):10-13.

Dixon, Marlene (1985). "Overview: Militarism as Foreign Policy—Reagan's Second Term." *Contemporary Marxism,* no. 10, i-xxiii.

Dominguez, Jorge I. (1980). "The United States and Its Regional Security Interests: The Caribbean, Central and South America." *Daedalus* 109, no. 4 (Fall):119-124.

Duncan, Raymond W. (1978). "Caribbean Leftism." *Problems of Communism* 27, no. 3 (May-June):33-57.

EPICA Task Force (1982). *Grenada: The Peaceful Revolution.* Washington, D.C.: EPICA.

Erisman, H. Michael (1983). "U.S. Foreign Policy and the Central Americanization of the English-Speaking Caribean." Paper presented at the Eleventh International Congress of the Latin American Studies Association, Mexico City, September 29-October 1.

Erisman, H. Michael, ed. (1984). *The Caribbean Challenge: U.S. Policy in a Volatile Region.* Boulder, Colo.: Westview Press.

Everitt, John C. (1984). "The Recent Migrations of Belize, Central America." *International Migration Review* 18, no. 2 (Summer):319-325.

Feit, Edward (1973). "Pen, Sword, and the People: Military Regimes in the Formation of Political Institutions." *World Politics* 25, no. 2 (January):351-373.

Finer, S. E. (1976). *The Man on Horseback: The Role of the Military in Politics.* Harmondsworth, England: Peregrine.

Fitch, John S. (1977). *The Military Coup d'Etat as a Political Process: Ecuador, 1948-1966.* Baltimore, Md.: Johns Hopkins University Press.

Gill, H. (1983). *The Grenada Revolution.* Mimeo.

Gill, Henry S. (1981). "The Foreign Policy of the Grenada Revolution." *Bulletin of Eastern Caribbean Affairs* 3, no. 1 (April-August):1-5.

Gold, D. *et al.* (1975). "Recent Developments in Marxist Theories of the Capitalist State." *Monthly Review* 27, no. 5 (October):29-43.

Gonsalves, Ralph (1979). "The Rodney Affair and Its Aftermath." *Caribbean Quarterly* 25, no. 3 (September): 1-24.

Goulbourne, Harry (1979). *Politics and State in the Third World.* London: Macmillan.

Grant, C. H. (1976). *The Making of Modern Belize: Politics, Society and British Colonialism in Central America.* Cambridge: Cambridge University Press.

Guyana Government (1976). *Joint Estimates of Revenues and Expenditures for 1977.* Georgetown, Guyana: Government Printery.

Guyana Government (1983). *Joint Estimates of Revenues and Expenditures for 1984.* Georgetown, Guyana: Government Printery.

Guyana People's Militia (1976). *What it Does.* Georgetown, Guyana: Litho Graphic Company.

Halliday, Fred (1983). "Cold War in the Caribbean." *New Left Review*, no. 141 (September-October):5-22.

Halliday, Fred (1984). "An Ambiguous Turning Point: Grenada and Its Aftermath." *NACLA/Report on the Americas* 17, no. 6 (November-December):20-31.

Henry, Paget, and Carl Stone, eds. (1983). *The Newer Caribbean: Decolonization, Democracy and Development.* Philadelphia, Pa.: Institute for the Study of Human Issues.

Hira, Sandew (1983). "Class Formation and Class Struggle in Suriname: The Background and Development of the Coup d'Etat." In Fitzroy Ambursley and Robin Cohen, eds. *Crisis in the Caribbean.* London: Heineman, pp. 166-190.

Holloway, John H. and Sol Picciotto (1978). *State and Capital: A Marxist Debate*. London: E. Arnold. Press.

Hopkins, Jack, ed. (1983). *Latin America and Caribbean Contemporary Record*, 1. New York: Holmes and Meier.

Hopkins, Jack, ed. (1984). *Latin America and Caribbean Contemporary Record*, 2. New York: Holmes and Meier.

Hopkins, Jack, ed. (1985). *Latin America and Caribbean Contemporary Record*, 3. New York: Holmes and Meier.

Huntington, Samuel P. (1968). *Political Order in Changing Societies*. New Haven, Conn.: Yale University Press.

Huyck, Earl E. and Leon F. Bouvier (1983). "The Demography of Refugees." *The Annals* of the American Academy of Political and Social Science 467 (May):39-61.

Inter-American Development Bank (1980). *Economic and Social Progress in Latin America*. Washington, D.C.: Inter-American Development Bank.

Is Freedom We Making: The New Democracy in Grenada (1982). St. George's: Government of Grenada.

Jackman, Robert W. (1976). "Politicians in Uniform: Military Governments and Social Change in the Third World." *The American Political Science Review* 70, no. 4 (December):1078-1097.

Jackson, Rashleigh (1982). "Statement Before the Twenty-seventh Session of the United Nations General Assembly, October 11." Reprinted in Ministry of Foreign Affairs, *Safeguarding the Security of Small States*. Georgetown: Ministry of Foreign Affairs.

Jacobs, Richard W. and Ian Jacobs (1980). *Grenada: The Route to Revolution*. Havana: Casa de Americas.

Jamail, Milton (1984a). "Belize: Still Struggling for Independence." *NACLA/Report on the Americas* 18, no.3 (May-June):8-10.

Jamail, Milton (1984b). "Belize: Will Independence Mean New Dependence?" *NACLA/Report on the Americas* 18, no. 4 (July-August):13-16.

Jenkins, Tony (1986). "Guyana: Electing a 'Comrade-President'. " *NACLA/Report on the Americas* 20, no. 1 (January-March):4-6, 12.

Jessop, Bob (1977). "Recent Theories of the Capitalist State." *Cambridge Journal of Economics* 1, no. 4 (December):353-373.

Jessop, Bob (1982). *The Capitalist State.* London: Oxford University Press.

Johnson, John, ed. (1962). *The Role of the Military in Underdeveloped Countries.* Princeton, N.J.: Princeton University Press.

Jones, Edwin (1981). "Role of the State in Public Enterprises." *Social & Economic Studies* 30, no. 1 (March):14-25.

Klare, Michael T. and Cynthia Aronson (1981). *Supplying Aggression: U.S. Support for Authoritarian Regimes Abroad 1977.* Washington, D.C.: Institute for Policy Studies.

Latin American Weekly Report, June 18, 1982; October 21, 1983.

Leiken, Robert S., ed. (1984). *Central America: Anatomy of Conflict.* New York: Pergamon Press.

Lenin, V. I. (1967). *The State and Revolution.* Moscow: Progress Publishers.

Levine, Barry, ed. (1983). *The New Cuban Presence in the Caribbean.* Boulder, Colo.: Westview Press.

Lewis, Vaughan A. (1982). "The U.S. and the Caribbean: Issues of Economics and Security." *Caribbean Review* 11, no. 1 (Winter):7-11.

Leys, Colin (1976). "The Overdeveloped Post-Colonial State: A Re-Evaluation." *Review of Radical Political Economy,* no. 4 (January-April):24-36.

"A Lovely Piece of Real Estate: Conflict and Change in the Caribbean." *NACLA/Report on the Americas* 18, no. 6 (November-December):19-47.

Lowenthal, Abraham F. (1976). *Armies and Politics in Latin America.* New York: Holmes and Meier.

Lowenthal, Abraham F. (1984). "The Insular Caribbean as a Crucial Test for U.S. Policy." In H. Michael Erisman, ed. *The Caribbean Challenge: U.S. Policy in a Volatile Region,* Boulder, Colo.: Westview Press, pp. 180-195.

Mandle, Jay R. (1982). *Patterns of Caribbean Development.* London: Gordon and Breach.

Manley, Michael (1983). "Grenada in the Context of History: Between Neocolonialism and Independence." *Caribbean Review* 12, no. 4 (Fall):6-9.

Marcus, Bruce, and Michael Taber, ed. (1983). *Maurice Bishop Speaks.* New York: Pathfinder Press.

Mark, Joachim (1983). "A Chronology of U.S. Intervention in This Hemisphere." *Caribbean Perspective* 2, no. 1 (Summer):10-17.

Marshall, Dawn (1985). "Caribbean Migration in Times of Crisis: The 1930's and 1980's." Paper delivered at the Ninth Annual Conference on the World-System: "Crisis in the Caribbean Basin: Past and Present," Tulane University, New Orleans, March 28-30.

Massing, M. (1984). "Grenada Before and After." *Atlantic Monthly* (February):86-92.

McKinley, R. D. and A. S. Cohan (1973). "Performance and Instability in Military and Nonmilitary Regime Systems." *The American Political Science Review* 67, no. 3 (September):850-864.

Miami Herald, August 11, 1979.

Miliband, Ralph (1969). *The State in Capitalist Society.* London:Wierdenfield and Nicholson.

Miliband, Ralph (1983). "State Power and Class Interests." *New Left Review*, no. 138 (March-April):57-68.

Millett, Richard (1984). "Praetorians or Patriots?: The Central American Military." In Robert S. Leiken, ed. *Central America: Anatomy of Conflict.* New York: Pergamon Press.

Ministry of Foreign Affairs (1981). *Memorandum on the Guyana/ Venezuela Boundary.* Georgetown, Guyana: Ministry of Foreign Affairs, May.

Ministry of Foreign Affairs (1982). *Safeguarding the Security of Small States.* Georgetown, Guyana: Ministry of Foreign Affairs.

Munroe, Trevor (1972). *The Politics of Constitutional Decolonization: Jamaica, 1944-62.* Kingston, Jamaica: Institute of Social and Economic Research, University of the West Indies.

Munroe, Trevor, and Rupert Lewis, ed. (1971). *Readings in Government and Politics in the West Indies.* Kingston, Jamaica: Department of Government, University of the West Indies.

The Nation (Barbados), April 16, 1983; January 23, 1984; February 11, 1984.

The New Belize, September 1982; October 1983; April 1984.

New Jewel Movement (1983). "Extraordinary General Meeting of Full Members of the New Jewel Movement." September 25. Reprinted as "The Alienation of Leninist Group Therapy." *Caribbean Review* 12, no. 4 (Fall):14-16.

Nordheimer, Jon (1985). "Ex-Belize Aide Accused in Drug Plot." *New York Times*, April 9.

Nordlinger, Eric (1977). *Soldiers in Politics: Military Coups and Governments.* Englewood Cliffs, N.J.: Prentice Hall.

Parris, Carl (1981). "Joint Venture 1: Trinidad and Tobago Telephone Company 1968-1972" *Social and Economic Studies* 30, no. 1 (March):108-126.

Payne, A. J. and Paul Sutton, eds. (1984). *Dependency Under Challenge: The Political Economy of the Commonwealth.* Manchester: Manchester University Press.

Pearce, Jenny (1981). *Under the Eagle.* London: Latin American Bureau.

Perlmutter, Amos (1977). *The Military and Politics in Modern Times.* New Haven, Conn.: Yale University Press.

Pitt, David (1984). "Belize's Longtime Leader in Crushing Defeat." *New York Times*, December 16.

Phillips, Dion E. (1983*a*). "Economic Dependence, Economic Growth and Income Inequality in Less Developed Countries: A Quantitative Cross-National Study (1960-1970)." Ph.D. diss., Howard University, Washington, D.C.

Phillips, Dion (1983*b*). "The Role of the Military in the Anglophone Caribbean in the Post-Independence Period: A Response to Crisis." Paper presented at the Eighth Annual Meeting of the Caribbean Studies Association, Santo Domingo, Dominican Republic, May 25-28.

Phillips, Dion E. (1985). "Militarization of the Caribbean." *Contemporary Marxism*, no. 10:92-109.

Poulantzas, Nicos (1976). "The Capitalist State: A Reply to Miliband and Laclau." *New Left Review*, no. 95(May-June):63-83.

Rand Corporation Testimony (1984). "Appendix." *Report of the National Bipartisan Commission on Central America.* Washington, D.C.: U.S. Government Printing Office, March.

Reagan, Ronald (1983). Televised Presidential Address to the Nation, March 23. (Transcript of speech in *New York Times*, March 24:15).

The Report of the National Bipartisan Commission on Central America (1984). Washington, D.C.: U.S. Government Printing Office, January.

Resource Center, The (1984). *Focus on the Eastern Caribbean: Bananas, Bucks and Boots.* Albuquerque, N.Mex.: The Resource Center.

Roberts, Michael Cdt. (1983). *Analysis of the Church in Grenada.* A secret report to Major Keith Roberts, March 15. Mimeo.

Saikowski, Charlotte (1986). "Reagan Foreign Policy Evolves Toward Center." *The Christian Science Monitor*, March 17, pp. 1, 12.

San Juan Star, May 5, 1979.

Saul, John S. (1974). *The State in Post-Colonial Societies: Tanzania*. London: Socialist Register.

The Scarlet Beret (1971). Journal of the Guyana Defense Force.

Searle, C. (1983). *Grenada: The Struggle Against Destabilization*. London: Writers and Readers Publishing Cooperative Society Ltd.

Searle, Chris, ed. (1984). *In Nobody's Backyard: Maurice Bishop's Speeches, 1979-1983*. London: Zed Press.

Sedoc-Dahlberg, Betty (1983). "The Surinamese Society in Transition." In Hans Illy, ed. *Politics, Public Administration and Rural Development in the Caribbean*. Munich: Weltforum Verlag.

Sewell, John W., Richard E. Feinberg, and Valeriana Kallab, eds. (1985). *U.S. Foreign Policy and The Third World: Agenda 1985-86*. New Brunswick, N.J.: Transaction Books.

Sewrajsing, I. (forthcoming). *Suriname in the East-West Conflict*.

Shak, St. Raffique (1971). "The Military Crisis in Trinidad and Tobago During 1970." In Trevor Munroe and Rupert Lewis, eds. *Readings in Government and Politics in the West Indies*. Mona: Dept. of Government, University of the West Indies.

Shelton, Sally H. (1983). *Testimony* before the Subcommittee on International Security and Scientific Affairs, U.S. House of Representatives, 98th Cong., 2nd sess., November 3.

Sims, Richard, and James Anderson (1980). "The Caribbean Strategic Vacuum." *Conflict Studies*, no. 21 (August):1-23.

Simmons, David A. (1985). "Militarization of the Caribbean: Concerns for National Regional Security." *International Journal* 40 (Spring):308-326.

Simon, Sheldon W., ed. (1978). *The Military and Security in the Third World: Domestic and International Impacts*. Boulder, Colo.: Westview Press.

Sital, J. (1981). Interview in *De Groene Amsterdammer*, May 13.

Sivard, Ruth Leger (1983). *World Military and Social Expenditures 1983*. Washington, D.C.: World Priorities.

Slagveer, J. (1980). *De Nacht van de Revolutie* (The Night of the Revolution). The Hague: Mouton.

170

Solaun, Mauricio, and Michael A. Quinn (1973). *Sinners and Heretics: The Politics of Military Intervention in Latin America*. Urbana: University of Illinois Press.

Stephan, Alfred (1971). *The Military in Politics: Changing Patterns in Brazil*. Princeton, N.J.: Princeton University Press.

Sunshine, Cathy, and Philip Wheaton (1983). *Death of a Revolution*. Washington, D.C.: Epica.

Taylor, Frank (1984). "Militarization of the Caribbean Basin." *Caribbean Contact*, March, p. 3.

Thee, Marek (1977). "Militarism and Militarization in Contemporary International Relations." *Bulletin of Peace Proposals* 8, no. 4 (December):121-127.

Therborn, Goran (1980). *What Does the Ruling Class Do When It Rules?* London: Verso Books.

Thomas, Clive Y. (1984). *The Rise of the Authoritarian State in Peripheral Societies*. New York: Monthly Review Press.

Thorndike, Tony (1985). *Grenada: Politics, Economics and Society*. Boulder, Colo.: Lynne Reinner.

Tiryabian, Josefina Cinton (1984). "The Military and Security Dimensions of U.S. Caribbean Policy." In H. Michael Erisman, ed. *The Caribbean Challenge: U.S. Policy in a Volatile Region*. Boulder, Colo.: Westview Press, pp. 48-71.

Trinidad Guardian. November 12, 1985.

Tudor, Cameron (1983). "More in the Mortar." *The Nation*, October, p. 1.

United Nations (1985). *Report on Human Rights in Suriname*. New York: United Nations, February.

U.S. Agency for International Development (1984). *Congressional Presentation Fiscal Year 1985: Annex III, Latin America and the Caribbean* 1. Washington, D.C.: U.S. AID.

U.S. Department of Defense (1983). *Foreign Military Construction, Military Sales and Military Assistance: Facts as of September 1982*. Washington, D.C.: U.S. Department of Defense.

U.S. Department of State (1984a). *Country Reports of Human Rights Practices for 1983*. Washington, D.C.: Government Printing Office, February.

U.S. Department of State (1984b). *International Security and Development Cooperation Program*. Washington, D.C.: U.S. Department of State, Bureau of Public Affairs, no. 116, April.

U.S. Department of State (1985a). *Foreign Assistance Program: FY 1986 Budget and 1985 Supplemental Request*. Washington,

D.C.: U.S. Department of State, Bureau of Public Affairs, Special Report, no. 128, May.

U.S. Department of State (1985*b*). *Security Assistance Program FY 1986*. Washington, D.C.: U.S. Department of State, Bureau of Public Affairs.

U.S. House of Representatives, Committee on Armed Services (1984). *Report of the Delegation to the Eastern Caribbean and South American Countries*. 98th Cong., 2nd sess. February, pp. 1-44.

Valenzuela, Arturo (1985). "A Note on the Military and Social Science Theory." *Third World Quarterly* 7, no. 1 (January):132-143.

Verhey, Elma and Gerald van Westerloo (1982). "De Nederlandse Militaremissie bracht Bouterse aan de macht" ("The Dutch Military Mission Put Bouterse into Power"). *Vrij Nederland*, Vn jrg (December):3-5.

Verhey, Elma, and Gerald van Westerloo (1983). *Het Llegergroene Suriname (The Green Suriname Army)*. Amsterdam: Vrij Nederland Press.

Waddell, D. A. G. (1982). "Britain and Central America in the Mid-Nineteenth Century." Paper presented at the Eleventh International Congress of the Latin American Studies Association, Mexico City, September 29-October 1.

Washington Report on the Hemisphere, September 24, 1985.

Watson, Hilbourne A. (1975). "The Political Economy of Foreign Investment in the Commonwealth Caribbean since World War II." Ph.D. diss., Howard University, Washington, D.C.

Watson, Hilbourne A. (1980). "Metropolitan Influence on Caribbean State Systems and Responses of Selected Caribbean States." Paper presented at the Fifth Annual Meeting of the Caribbean Studies Association, Curaçao, Netherlands Antilles, May 26-30.

Watson, Hilbourne A. (1982*a*). "United States Foreign Policy Toward the Caribbean." *Review of Third World Diplomacy* 1, no. 1 (Winter):15-29.

Watson, Hilbourne A. (1982*b*). "The Caribbean Basin Initiative: Consolidating American Hegemony." *TransAfrica Forum* 1, no. 2 (Fall):10-16.

Watson, Hilbourne A. (1984*a*). "Grenada: Non-Capitalist Path and the Derailment of a Populist Revolution." Paper presented at the Round Table on Grenada, Ninth Annual Meeting of the Caribbean Studies Association, St. Kitts, West Indies, May 30-June 2.

Watson, Hilbourne A. (1984*b*). "Merchant Capital, Transnational Banks and Underdevelopment in the Commonwealth Caribbean." Paper presented at the Conference on New Perspectives on Caribbean Studies: Toward the 21st Century and Prospects for Caribbean Basin Integration. Sponsored by the Research Institute for the Study of Man, New York City, Hunter College, August 28-September 1.

Watson, Hilbourne A. (1984*c*). "The Caribbean Basin Initiative and Caribbean Development: A Critical Analysis." Paper presented at the Pacific Coast Council of Latin American Studies Conference, California State University at Los Angeles, October 17-21, and published in *Contemporary Marxism*, no. 10:1-37.

Watson, Hilbourne A. (1985). "The Bourgeoisie and Economic Restructuring in Barbados." Department of Political Science, Howard University, Washington, D.C. Mimeo.

Weeks, John (1985). "The Central American Economies in 1983 and 1984." In Jack W. Hopkins, ed. *Latin America and Caribbean Contemporary Record* 3. New York: Holmes and Meier, 56-69.

Wiarda, Howard J., ed. (1984). *Rift and Revolution: The Central American Imbroglio.* Washington, D.C.: American Enterprise Institute.

Wolpin, Miles D. (1986). *Militarization, Internal Repression and Social Welfare in the Third World.* London: St. Martin's Press

Woodward, Ralph Lee Jr. (1976). *Central America: A Nation Divided.* New York: Oxford University Press.

World Bank (1983). *Economic Memorandum on Grenada, 1982.* Washington, D.C.: World Bank.

Young, Alma H. (1979). "Ethnic Politics in Belize." *Caribbean Review* 7, no. 4 (April):32-36.

Young, Alma H. (1983). "Belize." In Jack Hopkins, ed. *Latin America and Caribbean Contemporary Record* 1. New York: Holmes and Meier, 391-398.

Young, Alma H. (forthcoming). "Belize." In Jack Hopkins ed. *Latin America and Caribbean Contemporary Record* 4. New York: Holmes and Meier.

Young, Alma H., and Dennis H. Young (1983). "The Impact of the 'Anglo-Guatemala Dispute' on the Internal Politics of Belize." Paper presented at the Eleventh International Congress of Latin American Studies Association, Mexico City, September 29-October 1.

Young, Alma H., and Jacqueline A. Braveboy-Wagner (forthcoming). "Territorial Disputes in the Caribbean." In Richard Millett and Marvin Will, eds. *Crescents of Conflict.* New York: Praeger.

Ziedman, W., and M. Lanzendofer (1977). "The State in Peripheral Societies." In R. Miliband and J. Seville, eds. *Socialist Register.* London: Merlin Press.

Index

Adams, Tom, 1, 10, 28, 33, 34, 39, 45-46, 51, 52, 53, 58, 62 n.8, 63 n.12
Africa, liberation movements in, 9, 45, 125
Amnesty International, 76, 91
Anguilla, 32, 58, 62 n.3
Antigua/Barbuda, 32, 49, 51, 52, 54-57 passim, 59, 62 n.3
Antigua-Caribbean Liberation Movement (ACLM), 49
Antigua Labour Party, 49
Antilles Defense Command, 54
Arms sales, 53, 78, 81, 82, 97, 135. See also U.S. military aid
Arron, Henck, 110 n.1
Association for Restoration of Democracy (ARD), Suriname, 97, 103, 107, 108
Austin, Gen. Hudson, 86
Authoritarian states, 13, 17, 18, 22-28, 37, 39, 65-77, 81-85, 112-138. See also Military regimes

Bahamas, 44, 62 n.3
Bank, John, 46
Barbados, 1, 8, 9, 10, 32, 35, 45-46, 51-63 passim, 78, 88
Barbados Defense Force, 53, 54, 58-59
Barbados Labour Party (BLP), 46, 58
Barrow, Errol, 9, 17, 33, 45, 46
Bauxite industry, 128; in Suriname, 91, 97, 101, 102, 108, 109
Belize, 15, 44, 62 n.3, 139-157; British influence in, 139, 145, 147-148, 155; military expenditures, 140, 151, 152; refugees in, 15, 139, 146, 152-155; relations with Guatemala, 15, 134, 139-140; relations with U.S., 139-140, 145, 146, 148-151, 154; security, external, 147-149; security, internal, 149-155
Belize Defense Force (BDF), 147-148, 149, 151, 154
Belmar, Innocent, 70
Bird, Vere, 49, 56-57
Bishop, Maurice, 1, 25, 30, 31, 46, 47, 53, 68-76 passim, 78, 79, 82, 83, 87; assassination of, 14, 55, 65, 84-85
Bishop, Rupert, 71
Black power movement, 25, 44, 68
Blaize, Herbert, 46
Boodhoo, Ken I., 14, 158
Bouterse, Lt. Col. Desi, 92, 94, 96, 97
Brazil, 96-97, 120, 124, 125

British crown colonies, see Anguilla; British Virgin Islands; Montserrat
British Guiana, see Guyana
British Virgin Islands, 32, 58, 62 n.3
Budhall, Russell, 76, 82
Burnett-Alleyne, Sidney, 46
Burnham, Forbes, 25, 30, 31, 36, 62 n.9, 116, 117, 119, 122, 123, 128-132 passim

Callaghan, James, 53
Canada, 12, 22, 59, 61, 148, 153
Canadian Space Research Corporation, 49
Capitalism, 18-22, 24, 26, 28, 29, 38, 39, 40-41, 87, 89
Caribbean Basin Initiative (CBI), 10, 20-21, 37, 41 n.4, 148, 150
Caribbean Community (CARICOM), 71, 121, 136
Caribbean Joint Task Force, 1, 26, 50-51, 52, 54. See also U.S. Navy
Caribbean Peacekeeping Force (CPF), 33-34, 35, 51, 59
Caribbean region, as zone of peace, 60, 64 n.21, 136
Carrington, Lord Owen, 53
Carter Administration, 1, 9, 25, 44, 50, 52, 55, 143. See also United States
Cato, Milton, 49, 63 n.12
Central America, crisis in, 139-157
Central Americanization of the non-Hispanic Caribbean, 12, 15, 32, 145
Centrale 47 (C47), Suriname, 100, 101, 102, 109
Chambers, George, 10, 63 n.20
Charles, Eugenia, 10, 48, 51, 56-57, 63 n.12
Chile, 71
Coard, Bernard, 30, 74, 83-85, 89 n.1
Coercion and repression, in Grenada, 65, 67-68, 69-70, 76-77, 85; in Guyana, 127-128, 134; in non-Hispanic Caribbean, 14, 51, 61, 71
Cold War, see East-West ideological conflict
Committee for National Salvation (CNS), Dominica, 48
Commonwealth Caribbean, see Non-Hispanic Caribbean
Compton, John, 10, 34, 35, 48, 63 n.12, 89
Concessional Foreign Military Sales Loans, 35

174

Imperialism, in non-Hispanic Caribbean, 13, 17, 18, 19, 21, 22, 24-28, 39; U.S., 22, 25-26, 29, 32, 34, 37
Inter-American Treaty of Reciprocal Assistance, see Rio Treaty
International Military Education and Training program (IMET), 35, 149

Jackson, Rashleigh, quoted, 136
Jagan, Cheddi, 137 n.5
Jamaica, 10, 20, 36, 38, 44, 51, 55, 56, 60, 62 n.3, 68, 78, 135; economy, 8; military, 11, 12, 33, 35; relations with Cuba, 45, 78-79
John, Patrick, 47-48
Joint Endeavor for Welfare, Education, and Liberation (JEWEL), Grenada, 70
Jones, David C., 53
Josie, Peter, 49

Labor and labor federations, 12-13, 18-19, 22-23, 28, 35, 38, 66; in Grenada, 66, 67, 68; in Guyana, 131-132; in Suriname, 14, 90, 93, 97, 100-105, 108, 109
LaSalle, Rex, 132
Leoni, Raoul, 121
Lewis, Laurie, 119
Lewis, Rudyard, 53, 54, 58
Louison, George, 85
Louisy, Allan, 49

Manley, Michael, 20, 25, 31, 62 n.9
Martin, Atherton, 48, 49, 62 n.10
Marxist-Leninist ideology, 31, 72, 74, 83-85, 92, 94, 99, 106, 109, 136 n.1. See also East-West ideological conflict
McLean, Brig. Norman, 118
Mercenaries, 48
Metcalf, Rear Adm. Joseph III, 86
Militarization, in Central America, 142-145; in Grenada, 65-89; in Guyana, 112-138; in non-Hispanic Caribbean, 36, 45, 61, 112, 135; in Suriname, 90-111
Military, in non-Hispanic Caribbean: agent in crisis management, 10, 13, 35, 37; economic role of, 10, 117, 137 n.7; politicization of, 36, 37, 38-39; public expenditure on, 5, 11-12, 35, 61, 137-138 n.7; threat to government, 15, 33, 132, 133, 137 n.4
Military regimes, 2-3, 13, 90-111. See also Authoritarian states
Mitchell, James, 34, 60, 63 n.20, 88
Mongoose Gang, see Paramilitary groups
Montserrat, 32, 50, 58, 62, n.3
Movement for the Assemblies of the People (MAP), Grenada, 70, 72, 75

Nationalistic Republic Party (PNR), Suriname, 100-102
National liberation revolution (NLR), 31
Netherlands, 90-93, 96
New Jewel Movement (NJM), Grenada, 1, 9, 14, 30, 46-47, 49, 52, 55, 68-79 passim, 125
Nicaragua, 1, 10, 16 n.1, 78, 140, 143, 149, 156 n.9, 157
Noel, Lloyd, 76
Non-Hispanic Caribbean: attitudes about Britain and U.S., 29, 57; class society in, 19, 22-25, 27-28, 31; economic and social crises, 8, 10, 13, 37, 42, 44, 50, 68, 101; radicalization of, 9, 44-45, 49, 68; reasons for militarization of, 2, 7-11, 15, 42. See also individual countries
North Atlantic Treaty Organization (NATO), 51, 54

Ocean Venture '81, 26, 54, 83. See also U.S. Navy
Odlum, George, 49
Organization of American States (OAS), 64 n.21, 91
Organization of Eastern Caribbean States (OECS), 51, 53, 54, 55, 56-57, 88, 89 n.2
Ortiz, Frank, 47, 79

Panama, 16 n.1
Paramilitary groups, 30, 34, 38, 46, 58, 81, 112, 113, 135
Peace Corps, 148
Pengel, Jopie, 101
People's Militia, Suriname, 91, 92, 96, 99, 103, 105, 107
People's National Congress (PNC), Guyana, 4, 112-113, 119, 120, 125, 127, 131, 132, 137 n.4
People's Progressive Party (PPP), Guyana, 132, 137 n.5
People's Revolutionary Government (PRG), Grenada, 30, 47, 49, 53, 54, 62 n.9, 63 n.13, 72-83
People's United Party (PUP), Belize, 146-147, 150-151, 153
Perez, Carlos Andres, 122
Phillips, Dion E., 13, 158
Phillips, Layne, 76
Pierre, Leslie, 76
Pinochet, Gen. Augusto, 71
Police, as instrument of state power, 18; militarization of, in Guyana, 116, 128-129; in non-Hispanic Caribbean, 2, 27, 33, 34-35, 53-58 passim, 61, 69-71, 81, 95